# Your Show Will Go Live in 5 Seconds

## (Confessions of a Blog Talk Radio Host)

# Your Show Will Go Live in 5 Seconds

## (Confessions of a Blog Talk Radio Host)

## By Jon W. Hansen

ISBN 978-0-557-18344-9

# Your Show Will Go Live in 5 Seconds (Reviews)

From all my experience dealing with the media, I must say that Jon is best of class. After talking with Jon and then being interviewed on-air by him, I would recommend him to anyone. He is thoughtful, curious, affirming, intellectually stimulating, and superbly well-informed. I've come away from every conversation with Jon feeling energized and looking forward to the next one. I'm rushing now to buy his book, and I encourage others to do the same.

**John Ullmen, Ph.D. Executive Coach, Author of WHiCH BIRD GETS HEARD? HOW TO HAVE IMPACT EVEN IN A FLOCK, and lecturer at the UCLA Anderson School of Management**

I've done a ton of radio in my career as an executive coach, branding expert and author. Being on air with Jon Hansen is one of the most engaging, dynamic and enjoyable media experiences I've ever had!

To say you can learn about radio from Jon's new book is a total understatement. What Jon can teach you about connecting with your audience is truly life-changing. Read it and share your message. But only after you've done your homework!

**Libby Gill, Executive Coach & Author of YOU UNSTUCK**

Jon's book is NOT a technical manual on starting your own podcast; there are plenty of those available. In 'Your Show Will Go Live in 5 Seconds' Hansen shares his experience as one of Blog Talk Radio's most impressive success stories and how you can do it too! His focus is on the show and more importantly, on the audience. Jon tells you how to develop a relationship with the audience by facilitating a sincere connection with your guests. 'Your Show Will Go Live...' transcends podcasting; it's a must read for anyone who aspires to the major leagues as a talk show host on any platform.

**Jim Bouchard Speaker, coach & author of Dynamic Components of Personal POWER and Think Like a Black Belt - Host of the Black Belt Mindset PowerPOD show, JimBouchard.org**

I had the privilege of being interviewed by Jon last week. We had an interesting brief discussion prior to my going 'Live with JON'. What fascinated me initially was the fact that Jon was already asking intriguing questions, as if he had spent hours and hours conducting research on who I was, what I stood for and how we could relate. Jon has the unique ability to connect with his guests, from an intellectual level, emotional level, spiritual level and just plain down to earth level.

This book is a wonderful gift for anyone who shares the passion to communicate with others, on radio, on TV or live.

**Roz Usheroff**
**Leadership, Image and Branding Specialist**
**Bestselling Author of 'Customize Your Career'**

Jon's book is as informative and enjoyable to read as listening to his BTR shows are. I was fortunate to be a recent guest on his show (but before I knew about this book) and found our conversation to be one of the easiest and enjoyable radio interviews I've done. Not 'easiest' in the sense that it took no effort because there was a lot of effort expended by Jon prior to the interview. Rather, 'easiest' in that Jon did all the hard work beforehand to prepare me and then made it so comfortable and engaging to talk to him during the show. I can't believe the show went as quickly as it did. In no time, Jon was saying, 'Well, we're about to run over our time limit, Michael can you stay a bit longer.'

If you're serious about personal branding in Social Media and either want to host or be a guest on BTR, then you owe it to yourself to READ THIS BOOK!

**Michael Kreppein, Inquisix Reputation Network & Guest**

# Preface

Right off the bat you should know that prior to my first show on Blog Talk Radio "BTR" on March 26th, 2009 I had never hosted anything other than the occasional dinner party.

I tell you this as a means of illustrating the fact that under the right circumstances and within the context of one's own knowledge and experience almost anyone can be a BTR host. And it is for this reason that I have decided to write this book (that, and the persistent prompting of a loving wife whose most frequently used phrase next to "I Love You," "are you working tonight" and "no more garlic in the pasta," is "you know you should write a book!")

Now those who know me, or at least have had the opportunity to read my bio, may suggest that my "apparent" ease or comfort over the electronic airwaves is due in part to a somewhat lengthy speaking career. Certainly the opportunity to have the privilege of addressing countless audiences ranging in size between 10 and 400 cannot be discounted in terms of overcoming the initial hesitation to try my hand at hosting a radio show. That said I want to point out my use of the word "apparent."

While I have gained a certain degree of comfort in addressing an audience publicly, I can safely say that having to deal with the nervous anxiety caused by what I call the pre-podium butterflies remains to this day a standard part of my preparation routine. This has of course been extended to my BTR hosting experience.

In short we are all, to varying degrees, uneasy with the prospects of putting our self in the public eye and making ourselves vulnerable to the real or imagined scrutiny of a potentially unwelcoming audience. One day I will have to share my experiences giving a keynote address on a very unpopular topic to what can only be described as 200 hostile senior executives from the automotive industry - the term "pitch forks and torches readily come to mind." Fortunately, such situations are very rare as the majority of the people you encounter will honestly want to hear what you have to say.

The difference therefore is not in the actual experience, but in our own somewhat distorted perceptions of how people view us, or how we come across. As we learned in my interview with Dr. Larina Kase and Sally Edwards ("Death Before The Eulogy And Other Myths of Public Speaking" which aired on July 14th, 2009), this misperception means that we all have to deal with what Larina referred to as the instinctual "flight or fight" emotion.

Therefore the all important first step towards turning this as well other potential obstacles to hosting success into an advantage rather than a deterrent starts with acknowledging that there are very few of us who are natural born orators. The next step is to then remove the unknown elements associated with hosting your own show thereby creating a level of familiarity that transforms nervous hesitation into excited anticipation. The best analogy I can think of is the moments leading up to the point of building up enough courage to ask the prettiest girl in class out on a date - this is the nervous hesitation part of the equation. On the other side of this equation is the exhilarating feeling of excited anticipation after she has said yes. Well with hosting your own show on BTR, the pretty girl has already said yes as anyone can sign-up within a matter of minutes to become a host. Now all you have to be is yourself.

And like that first date, there are a number of things you usually do to get ready. This of course is where this book comes into play.

In the following pages that make up the 10 Chapters of "Your Show Will Go Live in 5 Seconds," I will share with you my experiences and insights in creating and hosting a show that informs, empowers and enriches your audience, your guests and yes, even yourself.

One final note, and even though the profession of one's faith is sometimes frowned upon in the realms of the business world, my faith is as much a part of me as my receding hair line and expanding waist line – all by the way, the rewards of turning "50" this year.

While the story in and of itself may very well have the makings for another book, my faith experience has seen me through the tumultuous journey from millionaire to pauper, and from abundant means to abundant need to a restoration based on hope and the confidence that the Good Lord has a plan for my life.

As I look back on a journey that began with an ominous knock on the door one Friday morning in May 2008, when a sheriff served me with the papers from an indirect business associate informing me that I had seven days to vacate our sizable family home, I cannot help but feel unencumbered gratitude as it opened a door to what has now become the greatest adventure and experience of my life.

So as you can see, regardless of your starting point or level of hosting experience, Blog Talk Radio is the great equalizer that provides us all with the opportunity to reach out and connect with a world that is as interested in knowing as much about you, as you about it.

It is my sincerest hope that this book will in some small way help you to walk through your door of what will ultimately become your greatest adventure.

Your show WILL go live in 5 seconds . . .

# Contents

# Chapter 1 - What is a Host?

*. . . a good host is "someone who always attempts to make the people around him or her feel as comfortable as possible."*

The word "host" has many different meanings. In the world of information technology, a "host can be a node on the internet," or a "computer that serves pages for one or more web sites."

The linguistic definition for the word host is "the preceding or following word to which a clitic is phonologically joined." I do not know what a clitic is let alone do I want to be phonologically joined to it.

Without descending into a definition frenzy that would make even a Cliff Claven shudder, I once heard a line in a movie where much like the "short and simple definition of a gentleman or a lady," a good host is "someone who always attempts to make the people around him or her feel as comfortable as possible."

The point here of course is that unless you are a hard hitting investigative journalist, or are part of a senate review committee, the most important attribute for being a good host and therefore creating a good show is to make guests feel at ease - both with you and the audience, and even to a certain degree with themselves.

By creating a comfort zone for your guest you are more likely to bring out their very best insights that will lead to a phenomenal exchange of new ideas and in the process add a different dimension to the subject matter being discussed.

In other words, an interview is not just an adroit exchange of questions and answers, but is instead the establishment of a true relational connection in which the listening audience benefits from the information gained through a stimulating thought provoking and yes, even entertaining dialogue between the host and guest(s).

There are of course many elements to making a guest or guests (I love shows with multiple guests), comfortable. We will discuss a number of the more critical points in greater detail in subsequent chapters however guest comfort is ultimately based on trust. Specifically, does the guest trust that you will be prepared with the right questions, or capable of responding to unexpected circumstances (in one instance a show prematurely ended due to an apparent lightning strike, in another example my audio was lost after the opening music). By the way in both of the previously referenced situations the segments in question turned out to be amongst the best shows I have ever done, simply because I was pro-actively prepared for any number of contingencies versus having to rely on an instinctual reaction to circumstances beyond my control.

What about pre and post-show promotion or, if you are doing a call in-show, taking the steps to properly screen callers before bringing an audience member and guest together on-line?

In the latter instance I can recall tuning into another show where the exchange between a listener and guest disintegrated into a hostile exchange based on personal character versus the subject itself. This is hardly the atmosphere which creates an open and sharing environment. Even though the guest was obviously experienced at being interviewed, it irreversibly changed the tempo of the broadcast as the individual's guard was up for the remainder of the program. Nor would I imagine that any potential future guests listening into that broadcast would be eager to expose themselves to the possibility of a similar experience.

This is especially problematic when you take into account the fact that all broadcasts are recorded and in relative perpetuity are made available on an on-demand basis. Imagine living that negative experience over, and over, and over again each time someone new listens to the replay at their convenience. (Note: BTR has recently introduced an enhanced switchboard that enables you to screen callers in what they refer to as a private screening room so that an off-air decision as to whether or not the audience member will gain access to the host and/or guests can be decided without affecting the on-air broadcast. An added feature to the screening process is that by simply placing the mouse pointer over the Caller ID number, the host will be provided with a brief overview of why the caller is on the line including their name. This is a premium feature that is available to subscribing hosts, but given the consequences associated with "blindly" introducing callers to guests and other members of the listening audience on-air makes it a worthwhile investment for this reason alone. There are of course other benefits including a guaranteed number of impressions promoting your show on the BTR site each month, as well as the ability to edit existing segments or upload pod casts for broadcast at a later date.)

Each of the above considerations collectively contributes to a guest's confidence that appearing on your show will prove to be a rewarding and enjoyable experience.

This also provides you with an idea as to the level of forethought that needs to go into every show before you even get to the point of going on air. In fact and somewhat ironically, the easier it looks to do a show, the greater the effort in the behind the scenes planning and preparation.

An example that will likely best illustrate this point can be found in the hit show So You Think You Can Dance. If you have seen it you will undoubtedly recall that before each routine, a brief snippet showing what the dancers had to do to prepare for what you are about see live is shared with the audience. Even though it only provides you with a glimpse of the level of commitment it takes to get ready for what amounts to a few fleeting minutes of an on-air performance, it doesn't take much to see that the level of success on stage is the result of hard, and in some cases repetitive effort.

What is also worth noting is that through the process the male lead gains the confidence of the female dancer enabling her to boldly throw her self into the air comfortable in the knowledge that she will be safely caught on cue and continue the routine to a successful and rewarding conclusion. It is this level of certainty that will enable your guests to confidently put themselves in your hands knowing that you will be there to catch them and thereby lead to the same mutually rewarding conclusion. In the case of BTR, a great and memorable show experience that will make both guests and the listening audience want to return again and again.

Now I am not highlighting the importance of advanced preparation as a means of dissuading you from taking on the responsibility of hosting a show on BTR. In fact quite the contrary is true in that in many instances the process of preparing for a show is as enjoyable as doing the show itself.

Think of it as preparing a great meal for family and friends, (I love cooking so I am using this example, but feel free to insert your favorite pastime here). Like a flavorful pasta sauce, there are a number of individual details to which one must pay attention such as preparing the different ingredients, and of course the timing as to when and how various elements of the dish are introduced into the mix. However, for many it is a fun experience that culminates with satisfying comments such as "what a great meal – can I have seconds?"

Like the preparation of a great meal, your enjoyment and enthusiasm for all elements of hosting a BTR show will ultimately be reflected in the end result – emphasis on enjoyment and enthusiasm.

Now on a side note, you may not be inclined to invest the time and energy to put on a show along the lines I have described in the previous pages. Perhaps BTR represents a fun hobby where you see the venue more as means of expanding your social activity, something like a party line on steroids.

I of course am not in the position to suggest you do anything other than that which does interest you bearing in mind that there is nothing wrong with a free and open format in which a few friends come together to share a laugh or two and have it recorded for posterity. As long as you fully apprise yourself of the terms and conditions by which you are granted access to the BTR platform more power to you. In fact if you view the Fox video interview with BTR founder Alan Levy you will note that the idea for the platform came about as a result of his starting a blog to both communicate as well as share updates with and about his father who was ill and living in another city.

This book however is focused on those individuals who view the BTR medium as a means of informing, learning, engaging and entertaining a broader and diverse audience.

It is within this context that the degree of preparation to which I have referred in the previous pages is hopefully meaningful and relevant.

With this in mind, the following chapters will provide a step-by-step outline listing each phase of successfully hosting your own BTR show. I will expand on key areas of the process including tapping into and coordinating your passion for a subject with those of your guests and audience without playing to individual interests alone.

I will also revisit the subject of preparation, but in greater detail, because similar to good advice it is worth repeating.

Other areas upon which we will focus within the framework of our outline include pre and post-show promotion. This is a particularly interesting subject in that traditional media has by and large been heavy on the pre and light on the post promotion of a show as the actual live broadcast represented the culmination of the marketing efforts. With your BTR show, the fact that it is available on an on-demand basis means that the live broadcast serves as the launching point for the real marketing activity.

Collectively the insights and experiences that I have gained so far in what is an ongoing journey will very much serve you as a position marker that will help you to do more of the things that work, and avoid some of the things that don't.

Even though I might be further down the road at the present time, once you embark on your own BTR hosting adventure, it is important to recognize that you have become part of a much bigger community of BTR hosts. This means that unlike traditional television networks competing against one another for ratings, BTR hosts are collectively making an important contribution to the platform's success. Therefore, as more people are drawn to a diversity of quality programming we all benefit. As a result I very much look forward to your "catching-up" with me so that we can continue down the road of a shared experience and a shared success, together.

# Chapter 2 - A Passionate Ear

*"When I think of radio I think back to the old days when I was young and radio was more than just an entertainment source, it was also a somewhat monolithic piece of furniture in the family living room . . . and I can also recall those Saturday evenings where I would strategically place myself below the legs, or under the legs of the unit and my Dad would turn it on . . . and that distinctive crackling sound of electricity pulsating through the tubes, and that distinctive aroma of an electrical fire although it wasn't as I anxiously waited to cheer on my favorite sports teams . . . what great memories."*

*Opening dialogue from the first PI Window on Business Broadcast, March 26th, 2009*

The above sentiments regarding my early memories of radio before it went electronic was an eclectic mix of sound, sight and even smell. Broadcasts of the fierce rivalry between hockey's giants the Montreal Canadians and Toronto Maple Leafs brought together four brothers (myself being the youngest), in which three cheered on the beloved blue and white against the hated Habs, whose only fan was my cerebral older brother Phillip. Looking back, it is clear that les Canadiens were definitely the team for intellects who had a deeper grasp of and appreciation for the intricacies of the game.

I can still remember the puck seemingly adhered to the sticks of the Montreal players as opposing teams made futile attempts to wrest control from the juggernaut line-up of the red, blue and white.

With the advent of television, black & white at first and then color, and cable and ultimately to where we are today – satellite TV with over 100 channels (although sometimes there is still nothing good to watch on a given night), the old radio gradually faded away into a haze of nostalgia.

Despite the passing of time, the memories are still as fresh today as they were back then. So when I accidentally stumbled upon Blog Talk Radio in early 2009 I could not help but feel a certain rekindling of that same passion that continued to boil just beneath the surface.

It is this very passion for a medium that did not allow your mind to tune out the moment your eyes tuned in that excited me the most about BTR. While the actual technology is different from the days of the snap, crackle, pop tubes, this renaissance of audio heaven is no less powerful than it was when I was a young child. This of course is the very essence that I wanted to bring to my BTR show.

Although the PI Window on Business show didn't keep score or count batting averages or track touchdown to interception ratios, I was determined to make each episode no less compelling. The best way I reasoned, was to provide a balanced mix of well researched subject matter with interesting and insightful guests in a high tempo format that would grab and hold the interests of a listening audience.

The challenge of course is in finding what I call the optimal intersection of collective interest. This occurs when those subjects about which I am most passionate converge with both the hot topics of the day and the ready availability of the thought leaders to be interviewed in the 12:30 to 1:15 PM time slot.

The trick of course is to maintain a balance between the three. If you focus too much on the hot topics of the day, your show will become yet another newscast. There is nothing wrong with delivering the news however it is a space that is well represented at all levels of media both traditional and new. Distinguishing yourself in the vastness of an over represented area of broadcasting is nearly impossible.

So while you definitely want to stay on the mainstream radar screen of listener interest, you also need to focus on subjects where your own unique insight can provide a perspective that challenges the listener to think outside of the framework of that with which they are most familiar, and likely most comfortable.

From a guest perspective, you want to be able to facilitate a discussion that stimulates a meaningful and enthusiastic exchange which makes each guest feel as if it were the first time they were being interviewed versus the hundredth or thousandth time.

In short, you want to make certain that everyone comes away from their BTR experience with the feeling that they have been part of something special, and that the investment of one of their most important assets which is time has been very well spent.

The first step towards this point of utopian convergence begins with choosing the right subject matter. A task that is sometimes easier said than done.

In this regard you have to ask yourself the all important question . . . what is my passion. Or more specifically, what subjects stir within me the greatest levels of interest and emotion. This is one of the linchpins for a successful show (the other being the Virtual Green Room which I consider to be the main or primary linchpin, will be covered in succinct detail in Chapter 7).

I know that many of us can talk about any subject with a combination of general knowledge and personal opinion. However, when we hone in on the things which get our motors running and our hearts beating in quick time, we seem to possess a natural aptitude that far exceeds any diploma or IQ score.

When we are passionate about a particular subject, our enthusiasm becomes infectious and like a strong gravitational pull, draws the very best from the people with whom we come in contact.

For me that passion extends to all areas of business, and the diverse and complex interactions between people and people, people and technology and people and the world around them.

As a means of feeding that voracious appetite of unquenchable interest I subscribe to a vast array of electronic newspapers, social network groups and online magazines as well as anything I can RSS (which stands for Really Simple Syndication).

While it does take up a good deal of my time – I wish we had 8 days in the week and 25 hours in the day, and can even be a little tiring, because it is my passion it isn't work. Not in the traditional look at my watch and count the hours to the weekend sense.

By being plugged in to a variety of sources I have the advantage of seeing a potentially emerging topic a little bit ahead of the curve. This gives me the time to properly plan a show based on developing events and not just personal interest.

For example, after benefiting from having two of social media's most interesting and insightful individuals as guests on the show within a mere two weeks of each other, my focus on preparing for those interviews put me in a tremendous position to both recognize and respond to a rapidly evolving story regarding the ever widening chasm between LinkedIn and its Power Connectors.

If I hadn't interviewed Shel Israel about his new book "Twitterville: How Businesses Can Thrive in the New Global Neighborhoods," and Ecademy co-founder Thomas Power about he and partner/wife Penny's new book "Know Me, Like Me, Follow Me" I might have missed the subtle albeit it prevalent circumstances that led to the July 28th segment with author and social media maven Neal Schaffer "The Gathering Storm: Has LinkedIn Policy Alienated It's Power Connectors?"

The added value of the earlier interviews is that a good deal of the research material and resulting discussions laid the foundations for the Gathering Storm broadcast.

That is a key "secret" to the process becoming easier with time. This is due to the fact that like compound interest, starting off with well researched information engages the guests to a greater degree. This in turn leads to further insights and information sources. The more insights and information sources you have, the easier it is to find quality material for your next show. Repeat this sequence of iterative knowledge gathering over several shows and pretty soon you are able to prepare for three shows in the time that it originally took you to prepare for one.

When I launched the PI Window on Business show at the end of March 2009 I was able to do one show per week (every Thursday between 12:30 and 1:00 PM EDT). By the end of May I could comfortably do two shows per week (every Tuesday and Thursday between 12:30 and 1:15 PM EDT). Over the last two weeks of July I was able to do three quality programs in a week.

I am now at the stage where I am booking guests at the end of July for 60-minute segments inSeptember.

Once again, I want to emphasize that this is not an Atlas holding up the earth kind of scenario. The fact is that BTR is just that good of a platform in terms of automating the broadcasting process to what amounts to a few basic keystrokes. Alright, maybe more than a few keystrokes, but you get my drift relative to just how easy it truly is to host your own show. Because of this you can focus the time and energy on properly researching the quality material that actually motivates guests to come on your show, and the audience to tune in either during the live broadcast or on an on-demand basis.

With the foundation of having a "library" of topics or themes in place – scheduling your show is a subject we will expand upon in Chapter 4 – you are now in the position to bring on a guest or guests. The only question is how do you go about meeting, engaging and inviting guests to share their experiences and insights relative to your selected subject matter?

While I have received e-mails from booking services or agents who shop around a stable of clients, I have shied away from utilizing these kinds of resources as they tend to commoditize the process which can lead to what I refer to as a "canned" on-air exchange that comes across as being somewhat contrived.

The reverse of this of course is represented by those hosts who in even the realms of traditional mediums such as television, ask the guests to provide them with a list of questions they, being the hosts" should ask. Surprising as it sounds, and according to guests that I have interviewed, this happens more frequently than one would suspect. The premise here is that the guest being interviewed will know which questions are the most relevant to their particular area of interest or practice.

In my personal opinion a good interview is one of give and take, where different lights of perspective are shined on a shared interest that stimulates the possibility for new and even exciting ways of viewing a subject. After all, the intrinsic value of the interview process is to learn or experience something new, and in the process gain a better understanding of a particular issue. With guests preparing their own questions this is a virtual impossibility.

As is the case with guests providing the very questions the host will be asking, booking services in similar fashion can also represent a "scripted" package that compromises the core elements of a successful interview by reducing the dialogue between host and guest to one of a unilateral broadcast. Specifically, the guest has something to sell and therefore has a set track of being engaged.

Now I am not suggesting that booking services should be discounted in their entirety, as for some they may represent (at least initially), the only source for possible guests. However, I have repeatedly found that the best guests are those individuals with whom I share a similar passion. While we may not necessarily agree on all points related to a particular subject, the discussion and even debate is often spirited and engaging for all parties including of course the audience.

The question you may be asking at this point is that while it sounds great in concept, how exactly would I meet these interesting individuals who are outside of my present circle of friends and contacts. After all, I may find Uncle Bernie to be charming and funny, but that doesn't necessarily mean that the rest of the world will share my opinion.

The key of course is to expand your circle of friends and contacts. The best way to do this is through the very medium upon which the BTR platform has been built . . . social networking.

Assuming that like me you have a naturally inquisitive nature encompassing a diverse field of interests, social networks such as Ecademy, Twitter, LinkedIn and even Facebook are veritable wells of potential guests. In fact, the social network resource has either directly or indirectly accounted for a significant percentage of the guests who have been on the PI Window on Business Show.

The key therefore is to plug into the various networks and related points of making contacts including groups, open forum Q&A's as well as the myriad of other engagement mechanisms through which these exciting new mediums act as facilitators.

However, and as discussed at great length in my June 4th segment The Psychology of Social Networking with author and co-founder of Ecademy Penny Power, bestselling author Patrice-Anne Rutledge and, social networking guru Andrew Ballenthine, you must view these venues as a means of making a meaningful contribution versus merely being a hunting ground to further your own interests.

Specifically, and this was a sentiment that was echoed by author and to whom many refer to as the Godfather of Social Media Shel Israel, broadcasting oneself ultimately leads to being tuned out by the general community. (Note: be sure to check out Shel's new book "Twitterville: How Businesses Can Thrive in the New Global Neighborhoods," which shares his insights on how the new medium is redefining global enterprise.)

What this means is that the methods you use to develop contacts, and therefore create the potential opportunity to meet or to be introduced to possible guests are a by-product of a service attitude based largely on the level of contribution you make to your network as a whole. In essence, you become known in your community through regular involvement and meaningful contribution. This presence then paves the way for either a direct exchange with a potential guest, or one that comes by way of an introduction through a mutual or shared contact.

For example, answering questions through LinkedIn provides the ideal venue through which you can make a tangible contribution while simultaneously putting yourself out there to both the individual that asked the question, as well as those who respond. Like Malcolm Gladwell's The Tipping Point, you don't know who is connected or linked to someone who might very well be the ideal guest for one of your shows.

This shared inter-connectability, much like the six degrees of Kevin Bacon analogy, is best summed up by Ecademy co-founder Thomas Power's belief (otherwise known as Power's Law), that "it is the people we don't know that are the most important." The only way to get to know these people is through proactive, mutually beneficial interaction within a dynamically growing network of contacts.

So what is the first step? If you don't belong to a social network then join several keeping in mind that there is an increasing degree of interconnecting links that joins one to another.

My suggestion would be (and in no particular order), LinkedIn, Ecademy and Facebook. The demographics for each will help you select which one or two will be your primary networks.

For example, the average Facebook member is in his or her twenties. They tend to be very comfortable with the social networking concept, and while there is a growing business presence within the Facebook community, you are likely going to find that activities are more recreational or socially driven.

LinkedIn largely serves the thirty-something crowd and is seen more as a business versus social community. LinkedIn is an ideal vehicle for individuals who are more "traditional" in their approach to meeting and engaging contacts, with the network being regulated far more closely than say a Facebook.

This image of a buttoned down, executive type was discussed in the June 28th broadcast titled "The Gathering Storm: Has LinkedIn Policy Alienated It's Power Connectors?" The show's premise was based largely on LinkedIn's arbitrary policy of limiting the number of contacts any one member can have. The restriction has its origins in the fact that the network was originally established as a means for professionals to connect with only those people with whom they have had a prior relationship.

For many both within and external to LinkedIn, the policy represents the antithesis of what social networking is all about. Or as one critic put it, it is like going to a Chamber of Commerce meeting and being told that you can only talk to the people you know. If that is the case, what is the point of joining the chamber (and in the case of LinkedIn, the network) in the first place?

The discussion (or debate) regarding LinkedIn policy is for another day (or show – do you see how show ideas can come from anywhere). The growing controversy notwithstanding, LinkedIn is still a tremendous vehicle for reaching out and meeting business men and women as well as authors and other thirty-something professionals. (Note: you will also want to take advantage of the Open Network service and group on LinkedIn. Costing approximately $10 per month, the service is designed to facilitate en masse an introduction between all members who are open to meeting anyone and everyone. I joined in the spring of 2009, and within a matter of a few weeks went from 1,500 contacts to more than 3,600 contacts – some of whom are amongst the most notable and interesting guests we have or will be having on the show.)

Founded in February 1998 by Thomas and Penny Power, Ecademy was created based on the shared belief that "there must be a better way for business people to meet, connect and help one another solve problems and expand their businesses. Appealing to the 40 something crowd, Ecademy (which is based in the UK) has grown to more than 500,000 members spanning 234 countries.

Some of my best guests have come through Ecademy including Penny and Thomas Power as well as the renowned Dr. Gaby Cora whose book "Leading Under Pressure" and related insights on achieving a more balanced life have made her a regular fixture on network television such as CNN and Fox.

While you may have your own preferences such as European-based XING and Viadeo, or North American-based Plaxo and Konnects to name only a few, I have personally found that collectively Facebook, LinkedIn and Ecademy provide me with the necessary opportunity to connect with enough people so that I could easily air a quality program five days a week.

BTR of course provides a good deal of assistance relative to inviting hosts and I would certainly not shy away from seeking their on-line tutorial help. That said when you do approach a potential guest I find that it is a lot easier when you have at least established a common relationship starting with membership in the same social network. In Chapters 3 (Like the Old Real Estate Axiom), 5 (An Advanced Track) and 7 (The "Virtual" Green Room), I will spend more time on the finer details of introducing yourself to a potential guest as well as demonstrating your ability to make his or her BTR show experience a positive and productive one.

Now, let's say that you have decided on a topic for your show, and through the previously outlined process you have confirmed the ideal guest or guests to participate in an insightful, thought provoking segment.

By the way, I think that it is important to point out at this stage that when PI Window on Business first began to air on Thursday's starting at 12:30 PM EDT, it was a 30 minute show. My reasoning was quite simply this; I would rather have something worthwhile to say and run out of time, than have all the time in the world with nothing to say. Similar to my father's words advising me that "it is better to leave the table a little hungry and look forward to the next meal, versus being too full and not enjoying the meal you just had," I wanted my audience to be left with the feeling that they always wanted a little bit more.

My decision to opt for a 30 minute segment initially was made easier by the fact that as mentioned earlier even after your show goes off the air in terms of the live broadcast, you can continue with the interview as BTR records and makes available all broadcasts in their entirety on an on-demand basis. Once again, this is a great feature and one that we will talk about further in the Chapters on pre and post-show promotion.

I also believed that a 30 minute show between the latter stages of the lunch hour would mean that listeners could tune in without having to worry about the broadcast cutting into their work time. Needless to say, running overtime by about 15 to 20 minutes each segment became a common occurrence. In fact almost all of my guests expressed surprise that the time flew by so quickly, and were genuinely sorry that we had run out of time.

The reasoning did of course seem logical . . . until I began receiving suggestions from listeners indicating that they would prefer a 45 minute to 1-hour segment, instead of having the show end prematurely. Using my father's analogy, the 30 minute show was like a meal where the plates are taken away before you have actually finished.

This of course is the perfect segue into the third and final component related to achieving the balanced mix I had referenced earlier in this Chapter. The first two that we have just covered are the identification of a subject with which you are both familiar and passionate and, finding interesting and insightful guests with whom to discuss said topic. Once you have the first two in place, which is reflected in what you believe will be a high tempo format that will grab and hold the interest of the listener you are now ready to introduce your show to an eagerly awaiting audience (re arrive at the intersection of collective interest).

It is usually at this point that I am asked how does one go about finding the aforementioned "eager" listeners. Listeners who will actually take the time to tell you that your show should be longer than 30 minutes?

After all, you don't want to throw a party to which no one shows up. Nor do you want to put together a great show with a terrific guest only to end up like a beautifully rare desert flower that blooms in relative obscurity out of the view of everyday life.

While I certainly had an advantage of a pre-established following through my Procurement Insights Blog (which reaches more than 300,000 syndicated subscribers each month worldwide), as well as an extensive speaking career that has become considerably more active in the past two to three years, where I am today illustrates the power of compound relational connectivity. Or simply put, fueling the domino effect associated with increasing exposure.

For me, the PI Window on Business Show is a critical part of what has become the PI Social Media Network. The network includes two main blogs, as well as a third Christian themed blog; the BTR show and in the near future a PI Window on Business TV Channel on Blog TV (see Appendix A).

Currently, through both unilateral as well as reciprocal syndication the PI Social Media Network can reach between 1 and 1.3 million people each month. The kind of reach that BTR has helped to fuel by recently making me a featured host across their entire network, a network that according to the same Fox 2008 interview with founder Alan Levy welcomes more than 3 million visitors/listeners to its site each month. (At the time of this book's release the number of people who tune in to BTR programs every month has increased to 4.5 million.)

The BTR recognition is just one example (albeit an important one) of what I refer to as a achieving a high level of conversational reach, which extends beyond the static confines of a single medium such as a traditional blog or static web site. Another example of how diverse syndication can prove to be invaluable in reaching an expanded audience is the Commonwealth of Virginia's decision to dedicate a page on their eVA web site to Procurement Insights' coverage of their innovative procurement platform. Besides posting all of my articles as well as the link to a previous PI Window on Business show, the Commonwealth sent an e-mail blast to 41,000 companies inviting them to tune in to the July 29th PI Window on Business broadcast "The Virginia Legislative Review of eVA Call-In Show." This is a perfect case reference as to the awesome power of the convergence of intersecting interests (re the balanced mix) between a timely topic, a compelling guest or guests (although I was both host and guest for the broadcast) and, audience attention.

Here is the compounding or domino effect . . . the invitations that many of those 41,000 individuals/companies received from the Commonwealth of Virginia may very well represent the first time that they have ever heard of the PI Window on Business Show. What this means is that we have been introduced to an entirely new audience of listeners, and by having access to the PI Window on Business Show site, they also gain access to one or more of the other mediums that comprise the PI Social Media Network.

None of this would have happened if I had not first had the Procurement Insights Blog (which itself was launched in May 2007). Because I wrote about a timely topic (public sector procurement, and more specifically Virginia's eVA program) based on a series of interviews in the fall of 2007, the foundations of a big audience for a show (The PI Window on Business) that wasn't at that point in time even a faint glimmer in my eye, was established. Now that they are familiar with PI Window on Business, and much like the Procurement Insights Blog, the BTR show will serve as a foundational launching point in developing an audience for either the PI Window on Business Blog or the PI Window on Business TV Channel.

Do you see where I am going with this concept of the optimal intersection of collective interest, and the resulting benefits of the compounding effect that occurs as your efforts begin to gain critical mass.

You should note that even though you may not be at the same stage that I am, prior to May 2007 when I launched the Procurement Insights Blog my social media presence was limited to a web site and little else. Two years is a relatively short period to go from a zero conversational reach to more than 1 million (and growing rapidly) syndicated readers/listeners and soon to be viewers. My hope with this book is to help you cut that two year time period in half. Over the next few Chapters I will show you how.

# Chapter 3 - Like the Old Real Estate Axiom

*. . . If you've ever been in the Real Estate market, it's quite likely that you've heard the phrase "location, location, location." As it turns out, property that has a good location has a much better chance of appreciating in value. Ray Kroc of McDonalds once stated, "My business is real estate." This may surprise those who think of McDonalds only as a fast-food restaurant. Ray knew that his company was involved in selling fast-food franchises however he knew that the location of the real estate for each franchise could make the difference between a winner and a loser.*

The McDonald's reference caught my attention based on the fact that we typically view the organization as being a "fast-food restaurant" chain. While it is that to be certain, McDonald's founder Ray Kroc zeroed in on what was probably one of the most important unseen (at least to most everyone else) elements of a successful restaurant . . . real estate location.

There is of course an undeniable logic behind his thinking in that having the best food in the world means very little if customers do not know about you, or find it difficult to get to your establishment. As stated, Kroc knew that the "location of the real estate for each franchise could make the difference between a winner and a loser."

Similar to Kroc's realization that location, location, location was a key ingredient to his restaurant chain's success, the "preparation" requirements in putting together a Blog Talk Radio segment has no less importance in terms of consistently delivering a high quality, high impact program.

I want to emphasize at this point that there is a definite difference between an autocratically canned segment involving the rigid and unimaginative exchange of questions and answers between host and guest(s), and a well established give and take format which serves as a touchstone to keep everyone on track towards achieving a collective understanding of the subject matter being discussed.

With the former, the purported track and timeline becomes the driving force with little room for any meaningful exchange. In the latter instance, while format is still important its primary purpose is to ensure that you do get to your ultimate destination while still allowing for a certain elasticity of spontaneity that can only occur during a real and meaningful discussion.

Often times, and without the proper preparation – which we will cover in greater detail shortly, some hosts work on the periphery of true engagement and insight by limiting interaction to a set of known facts and information sound bites. This usually leads to a familiar exchange of the same old questions that have already been asked on an innumerable number of shows by countless hosts. You will certainly get a response from your guest in this situation, but likely one that is equally uninspired and fails to deliver any new or meaningful insight. (Note: In a recent interview with bestselling author Shel Israel he told me that each one of my questions had at least five different layers of relevance for which there were multiple answers. Talk about elasticity and spontaneity.)

Asking superficial questions is tantamount to building a McDonald's restaurant in a location that is either hidden or inaccessible. In the case of a BTR show, relying on known facts with little preparation beyond a cursory review of the available information means that you have failed to provide your listening "patrons" with access to a greater level of understanding and insight into the topic being covered. The result is that a listener may tune in once, but will not likely return as there are endless media options and not enough hours in the day to hunt for your information location.

This being the case, why do people do it? Why put on a show that will not inspire listeners, some of whom may be potential guests or future sponsors, to tune in again?

For some it is time, or the lack thereof, and for others it is simply inexperience. In some cases the excitement of just creating a show masks the true effort that actually goes on behind the scenes to air a quality program. As I had alluded to in the first chapter, "the easier it looks to do a show, the greater the effort in the behind the scenes planning and preparation." So what is planning and preparation?

Think about preparation in the terms of the location, location, location axiom associated with the McDonald's real-estate example. How many people tuning into Blog Talk Radio each month would equate a program's success with a fast-food restaurant's decisions regarding real-estate?

This of course is where passion and interest, experience and research converge to uncover a subtle perspective that creates a unique lens through which an existing topic can be contextually viewed. It is the key to preparation starting with a great title for your show, "How McDonald's Real Estate Decisions Impacts Success on Blog Talk Radio."

If you read that heading for an upcoming show wouldn't the seemingly paradoxical elements of the title alone – McDonald's Real Estate and Blog Talk Radio, give you pause for thought and perhaps stimulate an interest to learn more?

When I spoke with BTR's Director of Programming Philip Recchia, who is himself a long-time veteran of the traditional media world, he indicated that amongst a number of important factors in creating a successful program, an attention grabbing title is one of the most crucial.

We are all for the most part familiar with the McDonald's brand as are we with the areas of real estate and radio. Based on the title, I would want to know how these three diverse subjects come together, and why it is important to me. This is the first step in laying the foundation for a successful show.

Now that we have an eye catching title for a segment on an equally interesting topic – how to plan and prepare for a successful BTR show, we need to go about the task of identifying and inviting knowledgeable and entertaining guests to participate. The question we have to ask ourselves is simply this, what type of guest would best suit our need to deliver insight for what is likely to be a highly interested and diverse listening audience? Would someone from within the McDonald's organization make a good guest? What about a real estate professional, or a Blog Talk Radio executive? Which one (or perhaps all) would you invite to be on your show?

It isn't a show about real-estate, nor is it really about McDonald's – although I am certain that we could connect with professionals who would be more than willing and capable of talking about these respective sectors or organizations. However, the relational elements that make the McDonald's real estate analogy a great reference point is the emphasis it places on the importance of taking a broader and perhaps unique view of the direct and indirect elements of success. With the restaurant it was a question of location, with hosting a BTR Show, the emphasis is placed on preparation. In this regard, the Blog Talk Radio executive or even an on-line host would be one of my first choices as a guest, although I would also welcome executives and personalities from traditional radio as well.

Now you might suggest that the show's title may attract listeners who might not be interested in learning the finer points of creating and broadcasting a radio program. In response I can say with great certainty that the topic of social media seems to be everywhere we turn. From blogs, to social networking to Twitter and YouTube, there is no shortage of coverage. Nor is there a limited or narrowly defined area of public interest.

If you recall from the Forward for this book, prior to 2009 the only thing that I had ever hosted was the occasional dinner party. If you had suggested that I would be hosting an Internet radio program before I had accidentally discovered Blog Talk Radio in early March of that year, I probably would have politely smiled, indicated that it was an interesting idea, and moved on to something else without ever giving it a second thought.

Similar to the old Alka Seltzer television commercial that prompts you "to try it, you'll like it," which itself has experienced a renaissance in recent years with Kathy Griffin reviving the catch phrase that first gained popularity in the 1960s and early 70s, Blog Talk Radio represents a renaissance of the old snap, crackle and pop medium of our collective pasts. That is what interested me, and given the opportunity to learn more about it within the format of an insightfully entertaining show, it will likely be of interest to most everyone.

You have now identified a theme (how to plan and prepare for a successful BTR show), created a snappy, attention grabbing title ("How McDonald's Real Estate Decisions Impacts Success on Blog Talk Radio") and determined from which field of practice or industry sector your guest should come. But wait, before you begin contacting potential guests, you need to write the show or segment description.

Serving the two-fold purpose of being a program guide for the audience as well as establishing the directional framework for the segment itself, the description will also help possible guests to gain a clear understanding of why you want them on your show in the first place.

For example, I might want to bring on multiple guests with one coming from the present day realm of Internet broadcasting, while another would be from the familiar world of traditional radio. Think about that for a moment. What a great show! Within this format you would actually provide your listening audience with both a present and past lens through which to view converging mediums. I can see the questions already!

Hyped up on natural endorphins and far too much coffee, the show description practically writes itself . . . and here it is:

Similar to the old Alka Seltzer television commercial that prompts you "to try it, you'll like it," which itself has experienced a renaissance in recent years with perpetual "D" List actress Kathy Griffin reviving the catch phrase that first gained popularity in the 1960s and early 70s, Blog Talk Radio represents a renaissance of the old snap, crackle and pop medium of our collective pasts.

Joining me to discuss how these worlds are now coming together through the exciting realms of social media, and in particular the conveniences of Internet-based radio, I am pleased to welcome a new media guru and a veteran of traditional radio broadcasting (Guest Names).

Both (Guest 1) and (Guest 2) will talk about the differences and similarities associated with the two mediums, and provide insight as to how one would go about creating a quality program that will draw and entertain listeners.

Do you see where I am going? You and I right now on these very pages are creating a quality radio program! When we approach potential guests, and passionately present them with our theme they will without fail want to know more.

To give them more however, you must also do your homework. This means that before picking-up that phone, or sending an e-mail, you should know something about your guest(s) to make certain that you are engaging their interests and strengths within an area of expertise that best aligns with the segment's objectives. After all, you wouldn't call your barber (I know hair stylist) if you had the flu. No more than you would call your doctor if you wanted a haircut.

Remember what we had touched on in an earlier chapter regarding the "optimal intersection of collective interest?" As a host, one of your primary responsibilities is playing the role of matchmaker in that you "marry" a timely topic, with a knowledgeable and personable guest. Then with enthusiasm through a well structured venue – you of course supply the enthusiasm – you engage and entertain an interested audience.

An important part of your responsibilities as a successful matchmaker therefore, involves extensive research on both your subject matter and prospective guests' utilizing a variety of tools including multiple web sites and Google searches. Besides obtaining needed insight, this effort will also pay big dividends in that the process will enable you to lay the groundwork to truly "connect" with your guests and ultimately your listeners.

Once you are ready to invite someone to be a guest on your show, there are of course a number of ways to initiate contact with them. In my experience, social networks or mediums such as LinkedIn, Ecademy and Twitter are ideal in that you are starting from a standpoint of familiarity . . . you both belong to the same network.

While I have had reasonable success with sending a direct e-mail to a potential guest, I have generally found the responses to be both faster and more positive through a network's internal messaging (i.e. InMail) system.

Another benefit of working through your social network is that the intended guest's profile page usually contains the majority of the background information you require either within its content or through embedded URL links.

In terms of your introductory InMail, you can certainly draft a version in your own words. However, and to serve as a guideline, I am happy to provide you with the following example (Example 3A) from one of my recent introductions/guest invites.

(Note: Blog Talk Radio also provides tips on inviting guests in the "How To Guide for Hosts" primer in the Host Tools section of your personal BTR account management page - My Blog Talk Radio).

**Example 3A**

*Good Afternoon Larry:*

*I came across your name through one of the LinkedIn Groups we have in common and after reviewing your site as well as your area of expertise I believe that you would be the ideal guest for the PI Window on Business Show on Blog Talk Radio "BTR" (http://www.blogtalkradio.com/Jon-Hansen).*

*As a featured host on the BTR Network, which welcomes more than 4.5 million listeners each month, I have had the privilege of interviewing business leaders as well as bestselling authors from around the world. Here is the link to the PI Window on Business Blog which will provide you with detailed information on specific segments, guests as well as a panoply of other interesting facts regarding the show. (http://piwindowonbusiness.wordpress.com/)*

*Titled"How McDonald's Real Estate Decisions Impacts Success on Blog Talk Radio,"the focus of the segment for which you would be our guest is on the importance of preparation in producing and airing a 60-minute radio show. As an industry veteran, you have been involved with traditional radio, and I believe that your perspective would prove invaluable regardless of whether the show is accessed through the audiences' AM/FM dial or can be listened to over the Internet.*

*We are now scheduling for the first half of October, and I hope that you would be available during the 12:30 to 1:30 PM EDT time period.*

*I look forward to your feedback.*

*Best Regards,*

*Jon Hansen*
*Host, PI Window on Business*

In my experience each prospective guest responds differently to the initial invite. I have had many write back indicating that they would be happy to be on the show, requesting dates and details. I will delve deeper into the specifics associated with providing the requested details otherwise known as a show outline which includes call-in coordinates, as well as the list of questions you as the host will be asking over the next few pages. As a side note, I want to emphasize the importance of providing every guest with questions in advance of the actual air date to enable them to prepare for the show. There are no Mike Wallace 60 Minutes-type surprise interviews. The guest is informed, empowered and enthused.

Alternatively, some prospective guests have asked to schedule a call to talk about the show and the expected format before accepting my invitation. There are many benefits to conducting a pre-show interview beyond the opportunity to discuss theme and format. Actually talking with an intended guest provides you with an opportunity to find out additional information that may not have been obtained through Internet research alone. In one such instance, I was able to gain further insight into the guest's area of focus which led to a mutual conclusion that at that point in time they were not right for the segment being proposed. Better to discover this important fact early on, than during the live broadcast.

I have also found that the pre-show interview process enables you to gauge the dynamics of the rapport you will likely have with the guest(s) during the on-air show, the advantages of which are immeasurable. In fact at the conclusion of these telephone sessions both myself and the guest(s) have usually come away feeling that our first discussion over the phone could have been the show itself.

Once again, the value of contacting a potential guest with a clear idea of the show's theme and ultimate objective creates that all-important level of trust that sets the stage for an open and informative interview. As the host and interviewer, it also gives you additional information with which you can better hone the questions you will be asking.

Regardless of whether you connect and confirm with a prospective guest exclusively through the exchange of InMails/e-Mails, or through a telephone conversation, once they have agreed to come on your show, the next step is to prepare an outline including format, timelines, call-in coordinates, and of course the all important questions.

The following example (Example B) is what I refer to as the Master Host Outline "MHO". I have italicized the question part of the outline that will be provided to the guest(s) at least 3 to 7 days in advance of the air date. (Note: the MHO is like a script in that it provides in a sequential order each stage of the live broadcast. I read the opening comments and guest bios pretty much verbatim, as it sets a sure and steady course from the very start. As I get into the actual interview, the questions are more of a guideline than a script. We will review the MHO in greater detail in Chapter 5 - An Advanced Track.)

## Example 3B

### *Opening Comments (Date of Broadcast)*

*Similar to the old Alka Seltzer television commercial that prompts you "to try it, you'll like it," which itself has experienced a renaissance in recent years with perpetual "D" List actress Kathy Griffin reviving the catch phrase that first gained popularity in the 1960s and early 70s, Blog Talk Radio represents a renaissance of the old snap, crackle and pop medium of our collective pasts.*

*But is a Blog Talk Radio really that different from traditional radio in terms of successfully gaining and keeping an audience's interest?*

*To better understand how these seemingly different worlds converge through the exciting realms of social media and in particular the conveniences of Internet-based radio, I am pleased to welcome a new media guru and a veteran of traditional radio broadcasting Alan Levy the Founder of Blog Talk Radio and the incomparable Larry King, to talk about both the differences and similarities of creating a successful radio program in the Web 2.0 world.*

*But first, the usual housekeeping chores to which I must now attend.*

### *Housekeeping Script*

*Now, for our regular listeners who are familiar with the show's format, this is where I usually talk about the call-in and live Chat Room access points through which you can share your thoughts and opinions while we are on-air.*

*However, and quickly approaching our 50$^{th}$ show, you are probably well acquainted with these great BTR resources.*

*That said every week I will take a few moments at the beginning of each broadcast to introduce you to some of the other fine programs that are part of the BTR family.*

*This week I would like to talk about: (Read Feature Sheet)*

*(Note: The Feature Sheet is on a separate piece of paper so that you only have to print it once)*

*Now, to today's show.*

*Guest(s) Bio*

*Note: as we have not actually booked a guest for our segment, I will provide the bio for the two individuals that I believe would be ideal for this program*

### Larry King

*Larry King is an internationally known American television and radio host.*

*He is recognized in the United States as one of the premier broadcast interviewers of modern times. King has conducted some 40,000 interviews with politicians, athletes, entertainers, and other newsmakers. He has won an Emmy Award, two Peabody Awards, and ten Cable ACE Awards.*

*King began as a local Florida journalist and radio interviewer in the 1950s and '60s. He became prominent as an all-night national radio broadcaster starting in 1978, and then came to dominate the airwaves when he began hosting the nightly interview TV program Larry King Live on CNN, which started in 1985.*

*Alan Levy is the co-founder and CEO of Blog Talk Radio. Alan created Blog Talk Radio in September 2006, after setting up a blog for his father who was dying of cancer. His blog inspired Alan to create a medium where bloggers or anyone can use a phone to create a live streamed event which is then archived as a pod cast. Alan of course hosts a show on Blog Talk Radio that covers all types of content including interviews with top authors, business leaders, bloggers, entertainers and more.*

### Segment 1 (Remembering the Radio Days in a New Light)

*Host Comment: Much like the Woody Allen comedy "Radio Days" wheneverI think of radio I think back to the old days when I was young and radio was more than just an entertainment source, it was also a somewhat monolithic piece of furniture in the family living room . . . and I can also recall those Saturday evenings where I would strategically place myself below the legs, or under the legs of the unit and my Dad would turn it on . . . and that distinctive crackling sound of electricity pulsating through the tubes, and that distinctive aroma of an electrical fire although it wasn't as I anxiously waited to cheer on my favorite sports teams. These were great memories that lead to a number of interesting questions.*

- *To begin, was radio really that magical back then, or as it become so with the passing of time?*

- *Certainly from a technological standpoint with today's digital TV's and Internet radio broadcasts in which everyone and anyone can either listen or in the case of Blog Talk Radio be a host, traditional radio is tantamount to starting a fire with two sticks. That said has technological advancement really improved the medium?*

- *Given the era associated with the Radio Days moniker, in which entertainment options were limited, was traditional AM (and then FM) radio more exciting and perhaps entertaining than today's high speed, 7/24 Internet version?*

- *In terms of making a personal connection within your own family, it seems that nothing comes close to a family gathering around the old Philco to listen to a favorite program or sporting event. I am having trouble picturing a family coming together around the "old" personal computer. Much like the family meal, is this part of family life forever gone? In essence, we may be "connected" to more people through the Internet, but are we any closer?*

- *From the standpoint of up to the minute (perhaps up to the second would be more appropriate) news availability we receive information in record time. Does this mean we are better informed, or does it mean that we are more distracted?*

- *One of the biggest criticisms levelled at the news media of today is that the race to be first has resulted in important events being either broken down into digestible nuggets that skim the surface of a story without actually providing any insight. In short, what is provided is information over insight. Do you agree or disagree with this position? If yes or no, explain why.*

- *While television is another medium, I can't help but feel that radio generated a similar level of excitement as did TV when it first arrived on the scene? With that in mind I recall the pilot episode for the series Happy Days (for all you trivia buffs, Happy*

*Days debuted as a segment on the sitcom Love American Style),
when Ritchie got a date with the most popular girl in school
based solely on the fact his family had a TV. Note that it was the
mere fact that he had a TV and not what was on it that counted
most for the girl. Would it be safe to assume that Marshall
McLuhan's the "medium is the message" was indeed applicable
with TV, and the radio that came before it? Is this statement
applicable to today's social media networks of Blog Talk Radio,
You Tube etc?*

## Segment 2 (The Quality Factor)

*Host Comment: Picking-up where we left off, the impact of the
medium itself in the era in which it was introduced was revolutionary.
Citing the Happy Days reference from the first segment of today's
program, the message was clear that just having a TV was more
important than what was actually on it. I believe that it was on the web
site of the nationally syndicated radio program Wise Quacks in which
Dr. Dave Hepurn wrote the following; "Not having a TV in my family
has its pros and cons. While we spend less mind-numbing and obesity-
inducing time with our noses glued to some senseless sitcom spew,
there are those days when we'd be thrilled to watch even the test
pattern on channel," I can't help but wonder if unencumbered
availability has raised or lowered the quality bar on Internet Radio. So
the questions I would ask are as follows:*

- *If it is in fact the case, that the medium itself is the message what
  role does providing "quality" content plays in terms of attracting
  and sustaining an audience's interest today?*

- *In the old days, with limited choices a listening or viewing
  audience would be more inclined to stay with a program, even if
  it was not necessarily dealing with a topic that was of great
  interest. Starting with the remote control and cable television,
  our choices have continually if not exponentially increased to
  encompass a virtually limitless number of options. With so many
  entertainment and news choices today and a decreasing attention
  span is quality more important now than it was way back when?
  Have we become more demanding by virtue of technological
  breakthroughs?*

- *In a recent article that appeared in The Future Buzz titled "How
  to Make (and Keep) You're Blog in Demand, Adam Singer wrote*

*"There was a trend for a while of people seeking more professionally-focused content from blogs. It is still around to a good degree, but my future prediction is this trend is going to fall the other way. The fact is now that so many businesses and industries see the benefits of blogging, they're putting tons of resources and time behind it. The content produced on their sites is clean, polished and professional. But what most lack is personality and character. That is an enduring trait of successful content-based sites and we will see a proper return to form in the coming years."* Do you agree with Singer's statement about personality and character over polished and professional?

- *What do you consider to be traits that are reflective of the kind of personality and character to which Singer is referring? In the context of the Singer article, how would you define polished and professional?*

- *Would it be safe to suggest that perhaps a successful show is one that effectively manages the balance between personality and character & polished and professional?*

### Segment 3 (Creating a Successful Show on BTR)

*Host Comment: The focus of today's segment is to gain insight into how an aspiring host goes about building a successful show. As a means of creating context with how the media has evolved, and the impact this evolution has had on several key areas of airing a program, we have gained some historical perspective on where we've been, where we are today, and where we are going. We are now at the "going" part of the program. To start, I would like to turn to you Larry and then Alan to ask the following:*

- *At the end of the day, does the medium itself really matter in terms of creating a successful radio show?*

- *Are there enduring principles for creating a successful, quality program that transcends both time and medium? Specifically, what are the core principles or elements for building a successful program regardless of the medium?*

- *Going to the other side of the fence how has the Internet including social media, enhanced our abilities to produce a successful program?*

- *Being in the media game for as long as each of you have been, what is the best piece of advice you can provide in terms of creating a successful, quality radio program?*

- *Referencing today's segment title "How McDonald's Real Estate Decisions Impacts Success on Blog Talk Radio," I am of course talking about the fact that preparation to radio is what location, location, location is to real estate? Would you agree with this analogy?*

- *How do you prepare for a show on Larry King Live, Larry? Is your preparation process similar to that of Larry's, Alan?*

- *Finally, if you had to sum up in 30 seconds or less, the key elements of a successful show for our listening audience what advice would you give?*

*With approximately 3 to 4 minutes remaining in the live broadcast I will ask you to provide any other thoughts you might have. In the last 2 minutes, I will announce upcoming shows, and remind the audience to check out the new PI Window on Business Blog, and of course indicate that the link to the On-Demand version of this telecast will be available as soon as we sign-off. We will also provide information regarding your respective books and web sites.*

*Additional Notes: if we find that we are running out of time, but are in the midst of a great discussion, we will carry the program beyond the 60 minute "live" broadcast. This means that the program will still be recording however the extended segment will be included in the On-Demand version of the broadcast which will be made available to you for posting on your respective websites.*

Congratulations, we have just completed a process that for many people represents the most challenging and time consuming part of hosting your own show – creating a quality content format. A well structured MHO, with great questions will stimulate an interesting, insightful and entertaining dialogue between host and guest(s).

As previously indicated, the italicized area of the MHO identifies the excerpt that will be provided to the guest(s) to assist them in their preparation for the interview. This information is forwarded via an e-mail which also includes the opening paragraph template provided below (Example 3C).

**Example 3C**

*Hello Larry:*

*The following provides the call-in details as well as an outline of the (Date of Broadcast) show - including the questions that will be asked.*

*The dial-in number is 1-347-326-9234. The show airs between 12:30 and 1:30 PM EDT, so I ask our guests to dial-in approximately 10 minutes (12:20) prior to the 12:30 start time. Once again it is the Eastern Time zone. (Note: even though technical difficulties only happen on rare occasions, I would ask that you maintain access to your e-mail as this would be the best means through which we can communicate in the unlikely event that we encounter a problem.)*

*After the opening music - approximately 30 seconds - and the initial general greeting, as well as a few minor "housekeeping" duties (i.e. listener resources etc.), I will then introduce you with brief excerpts from the bio that was provided.*

*As you know the show's theme is centered on the creation and airing of a successful Blog Talk Radio program. The following is an overview of the questions I will be asking:*

Now that we have a program with the right guests and an effective format to produce quality content, we are now ready to look at other key areas associated with creating and hosting a successful show.

This includes identifying timely themes and getting maximum exposure for your shows through the interconnectivity of the social media world. We will also review the technological aspects of airing a program on the Blog Talk Radio Network including, how to plan and respond to the unexpected such as cola on your keyboard, a lightning strike and a server glitch in one of the BTR switchboard servers that can turn a host into a guest in a matter of a seconds.

We will also review in much greater detail the finer points of marketing your program before, during and after the show's air date through blogging, video creation, social networking groups and even Twitter.

Then we will be ready to "Go Live in 5 Seconds!"

# Chapter 4 - A Theme to Remember

*"Thematic patterning may be arranged so as to emphasize the unifying argument or salient idea which disparate events and disparate frames have in common".*

In the previous chapters we have talked about specific show themes. Being "plugged in" to the world around you through various mediums and tools such as RSS feeds, blogs, social networks and the special interest groups within them is critical. Being truly connected enables you to gauge the shifting tides of audience interest thereby ensuring a steady stream of timely and thought provoking topics to discuss. This is what becomes the unifying framework through which story ideas and concepts will be filtered, and in the process establish the theme for your show.

Like the proverbial touchstone, your show's theme creates the continuity that links the "disparate events" of the world around you into a cohesive and coherent point of view. In essence a show's theme creates a reliable and certain context through which the audience can gain perspective and insight.

Now some might suggest that developing a show's theme should be step one (or in the case of this book, Chapter 1) in the process towards creating a successful Blog Talk Radio program. However, I am more inclined to agree with something I had once read about a performer who expressed their belief that "you can't manufacture a relationship with your audience." Even though picking a show' theme first may seem sequentially logical, I believe that you cannot build a relational foundation with your audience simply by creating a show. To really connect with your audience, you need to build a show around your passion and interests versus building your passion and interests around a show or show theme.

Take my situation as an example. I started out with just one blog that was created for no other reason than the convenience of having to meet a single, self-imposed deadline versus having to manage the multiple deadlines of the many publications for which I was writing. In essence, what has now become the rapidly expanding PI Social Media Network that includes a growing number of blogs, a Blog Talk Radio Show and a Blog TV Show was not part of some grand vision laid out neatly in a building block fashion. They were instead logical extensions of what I love to do which is writing, meeting and talking with people, sharing ideas and in some small way making a positive contribution to the world in which I inhabit. I did not consciously wake up one day and deliberately create a blueprint for building a social media network.

A similar example to which I can refer is Evan Carmichael who has been called "The Entrepreneur for entrepreneurs."

I interviewed Evan in August 2009, in a segment titled "Access to Knowledge: The Evan Carmichael Story." Excerpts from both his bio and the segment overview, tell the story of how at the age of 19, Evan became an owner and Chief Operating Officer in Redasoft, a biotechnology software company. The company quickly grew to over 300 organizations as clients, including NASA and Johnson & Johnson, in 30 countries.

With a stunning success under his belt at such a tender age, he started Evan Carmichael Communications Group and created www.EvanCarmichael.com with "the goal to give entrepreneurs the motivation to follow their passion and the strategies they need to succeed."

The EvanCarmichael.com web site is today, the Internet's #1 resource for small business motivation and strategies. With over 500,000 monthly visitors, 4,200 contributing authors, and 60,000 pages of content no website shares more profiles of famous entrepreneurs and inspires more small business owners than EvanCarmichael.com.

When I spoke with Evan and asked him "what was the real trigger" for him to start his namesake web site, he said "I wish I could say that I had a master plan when we got it going, but I didn't." Instead, and leveraging both his experiences and success at Redasoft he thought "why not share what he had found useful" with other entrepreneurs.

Again, there was no major plan to become one of the most dominant knowledge-based business resources on the Internet. The Internet simply provided Evan with a venue for sharing his experience and expertise.

I am of course not suggesting to you that Evan is not "grateful every day that the Internet exists" and that he can "make a business off of it," no more than I would fail to express my own gratitude for having a Blog Talk Radio.

What I am suggesting is that your first objective can't be creating a great radio show, because everything you do will be governed by that somewhat myopic goal. This means that your decisions as to which guests to invite to be on your show, what opinions to express or information to share will be filtered through a rating system that has little to do with providing insight and more to do with obtaining approval or "ratings."

As stated earlier in this chapter, a great show like a relationship with your audience or listeners cannot be manufactured. It happens as a by-product of a sincere desire to share and enrich, inform and empower those with whom you come in contact. Referencing the previous chapters from this book and specifically the point regarding the "optimal intersection of collective interest" if you successfully combine your true passion, with the hot topics of the day, you will draw subject matter experts and thought leaders into an on-air dialogue. It is through this convergence that people will be stimulated to tune in. Perhaps slowly at first but, they will listen because a sincere and passionate voice is like a beacon in Huxley's sea of irrelevance.

In other words do not create or host a radio show because you want to do a radio show. Do a show on Blog Talk Radio because it gives you the ability as the Internet did with Evan Carmichael, to extend the reach of your service and value to the community. This is why establishing a theme for your show is Chapter 4 instead of being Chapter 1.

So, what is your passion? If it is sports, then do a sports show. If it is as Blog Talk Radio Director of Programming Philip Recchia put it "a knitting circle in Indiana" then so be it. You may not have a large audience, but it will be a loyal audience.

Once you have identified your theme, the possibilities become endless in terms of potential subject matter.

With the PI Window on Business, everything from employee morale and the best leadership attributes, to the Buy American Policy's impact on the economy and "How to Argue Like Jesus" are within the framework of the business professional's interests.

In fact it is this very diversity that will enable you to reach out and connect with people you never even considered to be part of your indigenous listener base. Like the Power's precept that "it is the people we don't know that are the most important," beyond the surprise of gaining a presence in a new and unanticipated market, your extended reach will also provide you with the greatest level of satisfaction.

The following, which is an excerpt is from a blog post I wrote on September 2nd titled "How to Make (And Keep) Your Blog in Demand (The Future Buzz)," illustrates this point:

*"There was a trend for a while of people seeking more professionally-focused content from blogs. It is still around to a good degree, but my future prediction is this trend is going to fall the other way. The fact is now that so many businesses and industries see the benefits of blogging, they're putting tons of resources and time behind it. The content produced on their sites is clean, polished and professional. But what most lack is personality and character. That is an enduring trait of successful content-based sites and we will see a proper return to form in the coming years."*

As you will note, the point upon which The Future Buzz's Adam Singer places the greatest importance, is on the fact that while many businesses are putting *"tons of resources and time behind"* developing a blog, a good percentage lack the *"personality and character"* to establish a lasting and meaningful presence. This I believe includes extending one's coverage to take a more expanded view of the world as a whole beyond the framework of the same familiar topics and known relationships. For example, subjects regarding the effect of social media on the purchasing profession, or career path development and avoiding job stagnation are just two of the many areas that require greater consideration and attention. Even though these kinds of topics are not reflective of traditional supply chain fare such as vendor analysis and commodity indexes, they do recognize the fact that purchasing and supply chain professionals are people first. Or to put it another way, a reader's interest is varied and interconnecting. If you only address what amounts to a small part of your readership's overall individual interests, they are going to be spending an increasing amount of time looking at a variety of other sites.

The same principles are of course true for any medium including Blog Talk Radio. This is why the passion factor is so critical because it drives your interest and inspires your commitment to continue to learn and share more about the subject matter or theme upon which your show has been based.

It is also worth noting that at no other time has the market had as many choices as those within it do today, in terms of information and entertainment sources. According to Singer, this means that you have to "take chances" and, inject "fresh thinking" into your content. Specifically, if you are creating content in an "ultra-competitive category, you need to come up with creative content plays which break the mould." From a fresh thinking perspective, you also need to "interpret your subject matter through a different lens," by coming at it from an "unlikely angle." The strategy here, Singer concludes "should be to approach from an angle that the current players either haven't considered or simply cannot take as it counters their thesis."

Let's face it, we all view the world through a lens that is uniquely our own. While we may share similar ideas, like fingerprints no two views are exactly the same. So when I had emphasized the importance of being yourself in the forward for this book, it was based on the fact that you live in a "world that is as interested in knowing as much about you, as you about it." This brings us back full circle to not being able to manufacture the all important connection with your listeners. To be more precise, your audience is not tuning in to hear your show, they are tuning in to hear you and your guest(s) discuss a topic that is interesting and even entertaining to them.

It is YOU according to the thematic patterning definition that is the "unifying argument or salient idea." YOU are the common link of disparate events. Therefore it is ultimately YOU and not the show or the medium that provides the recurring theme that leads to the establishment of an ongoing and meaningful rapport with your audience. YOU are your own brand!

While we will go into greater detail regarding the subject of personal branding in Chapters 6 (Pre-Show Promotion) and 10 (Perpetual Promotion), I would like to spend a few moments on the importance of establishing a personal brand in today's electronically globalized marketplace.

In the segment description for my September 17th interview with national radio show host, author and Public Relations genius Marsha Friedman whose new book "Celebritize Yourself" provides the insights and tools you will need to establish a sustaining brand in the ephemeral world of social media, I asked the question "Are you ready to Stand Up, and Stand Out?"

It is an interesting question because few of us are proactively gregarious by nature. Unlike the politician who seems to have a natural affinity for getting out there to shake hands and kiss babies, most of us equate celebrity with being the unwelcome center of uninvited attention.

In reality, the opposite is true. According to Marsha, we are all celebrities to a certain extent within the sphere of our present world, and our personal brands are merely the extension of our passion, commitment and established expertise through tangible accomplishments.

By writing a blog, or hosting a Blog Talk Radio show, you are in essence committing yourself to the marketplace. Success therefore is not the result of celebrity, but celebrity is instead the result of pursuing your passion and sharing your message with the world. Just like Evan Carmichael.

Unlike the often quoted Andy Warhol saying that "In the future, everyone will be world-famous for 15 minutes," which has ironically endured beyond even his own celebrity, our fame is a by-product of our passion to excel in a specific area in which we have a natural interest or affinity. It is this passion that leads to the accomplishments and provides the creditability to be viewed as an expert.

As Marsha so eloquently put it, "you really need to have the creditability . . . you really need to have the accomplishments" that result from, and therefore "support your passion and expertise." Otherwise "you are going to be in and out in a flash," hence the 15 minutes of fame reference.

So rather than being captured and scrutinized by the uncomfortable rays of a probing and intrusive limelight, you are in reality operating within the realms of a world in which you are knowledgeable, credible, confident and therefore comfortable. It is within this context that you should view celebrity, and focus on establishing what Marsha referred to as a "sustainable" brand.

As your show evolves and yes even matures, so to will your brand provided that it is based on who you really are, how you really think and most important of all what you want to contribute to the world. Even if that world is within the relatively microscopic environs of an Indiana knitting club.

# Chapter 5 - Charting Your Course

*"The best way to get started is to quit talking and begin doing."*

*Walt Disney*

In the world of a Blog Talk Radio host, Disney's sage advice is reversed as we have to this point in time been focused on the doing (re "creating and hosting a show that informs, empowers and enriches your audience, your guests and yes, even yourself"). It is now time to "start talking."

As this book is not a tutorial from the standpoint of providing step-by-step instructions on how to use specific features associated with the BTR platform, I will provide a high level overview of the steps that I took to create and host what became the PI Window on Business Show. I would strongly recommend that once you have set-up your account, that you spend time utilizing the many resources Blog Talk Radio has to offer including the Learning Center, virtual tours, FAQ Blog Talk Radio 101 and even the Blog Talk Radio Forum which enables you to connect with fellow hosts. The links to these as well as other resources will be included in the "Welcome to Blog Talk Radio" e-mail you will receive upon successfully setting-up your account.

The initial step towards "Your Show Will Go Live in 5 Seconds," begins with booking a date for your first (or next) broadcast. For me and as someone new to Blog Talk Radio, this meant following their intuitive account set-up screens. Within a matter of a few minutes I was a "host" on Blog Talk Radio - easiest job interview I have ever had.

As I had indicated in the first chapter, I originally started out airing one show per week every Thursday between 12:30 and 1:00 PM EDT. While some surveys have indicated that the best day for a lunch hour show is Friday, I have yet to see any tangible data or received any meaningful feedback that would either prove or disprove this assessment.

In choosing the latter half of the lunch hour I reasoned that after eating, most people would be more inclined to sit at their desk and relax before resuming their work day. While this meant that I would likely have their attention, it also meant that the length of each segment had to correspond with the audiences' lunch schedule, which is the reason for the show's original 30 minute format.

Even though PI Window on Business now runs 3 to 4 times per week in the 12:30 to 1:30 PM EDT time slot, I would still suggest that you start off with a 30 minute segment once per week. This way, you will have an opportunity to ease into the role of host so to speak before taking on the expanded demands of a longer, more frequent broadcast schedule. Think of your hosting career as a marathon versus a sprint.

After spending a preliminary amount of time to become familiar with what the BTR platform has to offer you will want to set up your Main Show Page. My advice is to provide a brief description of your show including what it is that you have to offer and what you ultimately hope to help the audience accomplish if they decide to invest one of their most important assets – their time, to tune in to your program. While you will most certainly want to make the right first impression when you unveil your show to the world, do not over agonize about the description as it is a safe bet that you will make a few minor changes based on your practical on-air experience and corresponding feedback.

Your Main Show Page also provides you with options to upload an image which can be anything from your best head shot, to company logo or for that matter any image that symbolizes the nature and intent of your program.

The Show Page also provides places where you can insert videos, presentation material as well as links back to your web site or blog. Blogs by the way are an integral part of the show experience, so if you have one be certain to incorporate it into what should be a collaborative venue for your listeners or readership. We will of course discuss blogs in greater detail in Chapters 6 (Pre-Show Promotion), 9 (Reviewing the Game Film) and, 10 (Perpetual Promotion), including syndicated posting through applications such as Ping.fm.

If you do not have a blog I would urge you to start one prior to your next air date as it is an invaluable medium in so many ways including pre and post show promotion as well as segment commentaries. I personally use WordPress and based on what I have seen it appears to be one of the top, if not the top blog sites in the industry offering ease of use with increasing functionality through third-party format themes and some pretty cool widgets.

When you have set-up your account and your Main Show Page, you are now officially ready to book your first air date.

Once again, the day and time for you to reach the maximum number of people from your targeted audience will vary. For example, if your show is focused on helping stay at home moms or dads with everyday challenges from getting the kids ready for school, to preparing the right kinds of lunch to balancing the check book and selecting the right dinner menu you are more than likely going find your biggest audience during periods of downtime. Perhaps at 10:30 in the morning, when the toddler is having his or her nap and Mom or Dad has recovered from the morning rush.

Conversely, if you are providing a show geared toward teachers, the daytime hours – with the exception of perhaps lunchtime – would not be good as they are more than likely teaching a class at that time.

Ultimately, you are the best one to determine the day and time that will be most suitable for your targeted audience. The above examples are merely designed to point you in the right direction relative to what you should be considering.

I would be remiss if I did not highlight one of the greatest features of Blog Talk Radio which is the fact that all programs are recorded and made available on an on-demand basis. This means that if your listeners cannot tune in to the "live" broadcast, they can still listen to the segment at their convenience through the on-demand link or player.

We will be discussing the on-demand player feature in greater detail in the chapter dealing with perpetual marketing, including how distribution of a player can turn both individual segments and your show in general into a viral phenomenon.

Unlike traditional radio where repeat broadcasts are still subject to someone other than the listener's schedule, BTR's on-demand player opens up the possibility to build your audience much faster by adapting to the time demands of each individual listener.

However, even though this amazing feature is available to accommodate anyone's schedule, it still does not lessen the importance of choosing the right day and time slot for your show. In essence, the consistency of your live broadcast schedule creates a certainty of your reliable and ongoing availability that tells the listener you are one of the shows worth following because you are in it for the long haul.

Consistency is without fail one of the most critical tenets of being the host of a successful program. This includes answering the proverbial call without fail each and every week at the appointed time.

The best examples I can provide as a means of illustrating the importance of consistency relative to scheduling is television. Some of the best and most entertaining shows have been lost because of what I call nomadic scheduling practices.

Take ABC's Sports Night. The sitcom featured a first rate cast that included Felicity Huffman (now of Desperate Housewives), Peter Krause (who later went on to star in the HBO smash hit Six Feet Under) and Robert Guillaume (of "Benson" fame). Despite topping the critic's list during its two year run Sports Night according to MSN Entertainment's Dave McCoy, "was hard to find during its second season, and then simply disappeared."

I am certain that you probably have your own list of shows that you have enjoyed and believe should still be occupying the television air waves. For want of a home in terms of a set broadcast day and time, they might still be on the air today. This of course is entirely my point.

Hosting your own show on Blog Talk Radio means being there when you say you are going to be there.

There is of course going to be times that you may not be able to make a scheduled broadcast due to illness, emergencies, last minute guest cancellations or even taking a planned two week vacation. In theses circumstances Blog Talk Radio has recognized the importance of providing its hosts with a contingency planning capability, including an option to easily upload a previous segment or pod cast so your listeners are not greeted by silence when they tune in. You will of course want to update your BTR segment page to reflect the change, adding that the show originally scheduled to air at that time will be re-scheduled for a later date, and that the listener should visit your blog and/or main show page for updates.

In those instances where a change has to be made on the day the program is scheduled to air or, just moments before going live – I must admit that despite sending the show's outline to guests well in advance of the air date, I am always a little uneasy about technical problems or situations where for whatever reason the guest might not be not able to call-in at the appointed time - I always have a back-up plan. This includes a host only segment outline including specific topics that can still deliver a great show if you find yourself having to fly solo. (Note: As the host, you will usually call-in 15 minutes prior to air time. If the guest or guests for a particular segment have not dialled-in by the 10 minute to air-time mark, I send out an e-mail reminding them that the show will be starting soon and provide them with the call-in number. I also include a personal "Have a great show" note of encouragement. One additional consideration regarding contingency planning on the day of a show is to make certain that you instruct your guests to have ready access to their e-mail. There have been several instances where technical difficulties have left e-mail as the only way to communicate with a guest to bring them back on-line quickly.)

In those instances where you discover the need to make a change several days or longer in advance of the scheduled broadcast, social media venues such as LinkedIn, Twitter and your blog will provide you with the ability to get the word out to your audience quickly and reliably.

Turning our attention back to scheduling your first show, and referencing the steps that have been laid out in the previous chapters you will not find yourself in need of ideas relating to a possible theme. While I will leave it to your own good judgment as to what the show will be about, I would like to suggest that the first broadcast be used as a means of introducing yourself to the audience without the distraction of a guest or thought-provoking topic.

The first PI Window on Business show was a 30 minute getting to know you affair in which I talked with my audience about my background and my previous experiences with radio. I shared with them my intentions for the show and what I hoped to deliver to them week in and week out. Basically, I wanted them to get to know me personally, and to gain a better understanding of why I was asking them to invest 30 minutes of their time each week to tune in.

(Note: If you are a current Blog Talk Radio host who broadcasts on a regular basis you have probably purchased this book more as a means of fine tuning your already successful program. If this is the case, then much like a buffet I will leave it to your discretion as to what you choose to put on your plate and take back to the table – or broadcast seat in this instance.)

Beyond the first show, and if you are starting with one broadcast per week, you should at minimum have the following two week period booked – although my personal preference is to have at least four weeks scheduled in advance.

Besides demonstrating your commitment to doing a show, having advanced bookings will enable you to properly market each segment to potential listeners so that they can begin to plan their schedules accordingly. Another neat BTR feature provides interested listeners with an ability to send a reminder to their on-line calendar directly from your Main Show Page. This means that they will be automatically prompted to tune in on the day the segment is going to air.

On the day your segment will air, your prior preparation as outlined in Chapter 3 will mean that there should be little to do other than a few last minute details including one or two "run throughs" of the show outline. The result being that you will be free to focus on the other areas of your business (for me writing this book, managing sponsor commitments, posting blogs etc.), and of course the show itself. In essence, and resulting from taking the time establish an effective preparation routine up front, you will be relaxed and ready to host a great show!

One final piece of advice that I feel is important to share deals with technological awareness and the unexpected.

The unexpected can involve anything from lightning strikes to spilled coffee (or cola) on your keyboard or a glitch in the main BTR switchboard that kicks you out as the host of your own show and will not allow you to dial back in.

Regarding the last point, I will share the following excerpt from a post I had made in the BTR Guest Resource Group on Inquisix:

*Your 9 minutes into your show and suddenly a voice comes over the line telling you that the host (which is you) has already called-in, and that you will now be disconnected. What do you do?*

*I found myself in that very situation yesterday and discovered (on the fly) that you can still conduct your interview through the guest call-in number.*

*The following outlines the circumstances surrounding the challenge, the resolution and what BTR is doing to avoid similar occurrences in the future. (Note: BTR's response to my service report was both fast and courteous.)*

*Details:*

*My show, the PI Window on Business aired today at 12:30 PM EDT.*

*The guest had difficulty with calling-in (he kept getting disconnected).*

*I hung-up and logged out of the BTR System, then both logged and called back in again . . . just in time for going live on the air.*

*About 9 minutes into the show, a voice came over my phone telling me that the host had already called-in, and I was disconnected. My phone number however continued to be displayed in the host section of the switchboard indicating that I was still on-line.*

*I attempted to call-in using the host number, but was denied access.*

*The only logical thought I had was to call-in using the guest number. I did, and thankfully was able to talk with my guest, as well as confirm through the Chat Room that listeners could indeed hear the show.*

*This all happened within the space of a 1 to 2 minute window, so interestingly enough we did not appear to miss a beat (Note: we had dead air for 3 minutes, which of course will be edited out of the segment).*

*By the way, I was still able to control the host switchboard through the guest call-in number including activating the closing music.*

Even though the above scenario presented a few problems, being familiar with the BTR platform meant that I had the ability to think quickly without a major disruption of what turned out to be a great show.

The key is that through a combination of knowing what options were available to me from a technological standpoint, as well as maintaining a cool head, the difficulties became an interesting footnote to a terrific interview instead of a show stopper.

It is also important to remember to keep your cool. No matter what happens, when you encounter a problem know that you are probably not the first host to ever experience the same hiccup in one form or another such as spilling your beverage.

I can remember during one broadcast knocking over an entire glass of cola with my hand and having the contents bath my keyboard, desk and of course yours truly with what quickly became a sticky mess. Seeing that it wasn't TV (although I am certain if it had been, it would have inspired a chuckle or two), and having at my ready disposal tissues and hand sanitizer I continued with the interview as if nothing had happened.

In fact if you listen to the episode in question (Linking Opportunities with Result: Getting LinkedIn in 10 Minutes, August 18th, 2009), you would be hard pressed to determine where in the broadcast this major spillage occurred.

That of course is my point. Despite the best laid plans things can and do happen. You can't prevent it. How you respond to these quirky turns of everyday life is what is important. Planning and preparation will go a long ways in helping you to effectively and seamlessly deal with most things that you will encounter in your experiences as a Blog Talk Radio Host.

Regarding those situations for which no amount of planning or preparation will help, just remember one thing . . . we are all human and therefore we have all had our moments. So relax, go with the flow and with all humility and even humour do your best to get back on track.

# Chapter 6 - Pre-Show Promotion

*...means arranging various media to help each other so they won't cancel each other out, to buttress one medium with another. You might say, for example, that radio is a bigger help to literacy than television, but television might be a very wonderful aid to teaching languages. And so you can do some things on some media that you cannot do on others. And, therefore, if you watch the whole field, you can prevent this waste that comes by one cancelling the other out.*

*Marshall McLuhan on media ecology, 1977*

Recently and quite frequently I have found myself in discussions with a variety of individuals and organizations who contact me regarding sponsorship of the PI Social Media Network's various mediums. This includes the PI Window on Business Show on Blog Talk Radio, the Procurement Insights and PI Window on Business Blogs and the soon to be launched PI Inquisitive Eye and TV2 Young Entrepreneurs TV Channels.

Over the past twelve months, I have noticed a marked decline in the request for information relative to site visits in which there is an attempt to artificially confine readers or listeners to a single URL address. I have instead seen a growing interest in areas such as relational or conversational marketing in which as McLuhan observed "means arranging various media to help each other." This at its very essence is representative of the social media phenomenon.

What you need to ask yourself is one simple question . . . "Am I in the social media picture?"

To help you to gain a better understanding of what this questions really means, and therefore answer it with a high degree of certainty it is important to recognize the differences between promotion under a traditional broadcasting model, and promotion in the realm of the social media world.

As a first step in this exercise of understanding I am going to share with you an excerpt from a blog post I wrote recently for a PI

Window on Business segment titled "Me lookin at you and you lookin at me: Staging Social Network Advertising."

*"Just as I thought it was goin alright I found out how wrong when I thought I was right, It's always the same its just a shame that's all*

*I could say day, and you'd say night, Tell me it's black when I know that's its white It's always the same it's just a shame that's all!"*

For those of us who remember the mid-eighties and in particular Phil Collins' run of hits the above lyrics will be familiar.

The tie-in to the above segment is that talking does not mean connecting. Sending out a message does not mean it is being received.

When I first viewed David Cushman's SlideShare presentation titled "Why Traditional Ad Models will not work in social networks (and what will...)," I was immediately caught by both the succinctness of the message (it is only 10 slides long) and the significance of its meaning. A meaning, which given the fact that I had just published a series of articles on the viability of social media models, took on added significance based on the prediction of industry veteran J. William Grimes that the daily newspaper would no longer be in existence in 5 years.

Unlike traditional advertising in which the number of eyeballs looking toward what Cushman referred to as a stage is the critical point of connection, social networking as the refrain from the Collins song goes is "Me lookin at you and you lookin at me."

The trouble is that most companies whether large or small do not really grasp what this direct one-to-one connection means and what it really involves . . . "Turnin me on, turnin me off" is more often that not the end result.

Like it or not, social networking has redefined how we interact and do business.

The above post served the dual purpose of promoting the PI Window on Business segment, but in a broader sense it highlighted what is often the first and usually misdirected step in terms of promoting one's show.

What Cushman was referring to is the reality that people no longer centrally converge in a single, large meeting place where their focus is on a single venue or stage. Instead, in the smaller community driven world of social networking the message is carried from one group to another by individuals building the kind of critical mass to which Malcolm Gladwell referenced in his bestselling book "The Tipping Point." Little things it turns out can make a big difference!

When Gladwell talked about social epidemics (an analogy that was both brilliant and prophetic given that his book was released in 2000 - long before the majority of us were even aware of the concept of social networking), he tapped into the true power of social media and conversational marketing.

To illustrate his point, Gladwell pointed out the fact that a single child with the measles "virus" could trigger and outbreak of the illness within his or her entire classroom that could then spread throughout the entire school and then to the community as a whole. You see where I am going with this train of thought.

What Gladwell realized is that a single individual could cause a chain reaction of enormous and unexpected proportion through contact within his or her close and relatively small circle of influence. Cushman's presentation illustrated the point that the many-to-one broadcast model associated with traditional advertising presents little opportunity to establish this necessary and personal connection with an individual influencer.

Therefore, when you look at promoting your show how do you establish this all important connection with individual influencers? How do you connect with those people to whom Gladwell refers to as the "Connectors, Mavens, and Salesmen?" How do you get to the stage of "Me lookin at you and you lookin at me?"

The purpose of this chapter is to answer this (as well as other) questions.

The Syndicated Network Concept provides a collective and collaborative framework for "arranging various media to help each other," by recognizing the fact that a single venue or landing point even if site hits are growing represents a declining sphere of market reach and influence.

In other words, and with the advent of social media, it is no longer critical to have individual and siloed web sites competing for the eyes, ears and minds of the reader, listener or viewer. Under this scenario you are trying to quantify market interest through a single domain ranking versus extending your message, service, postulations or prognostications through inter-connecting groups and communities. It is similar to the story of the giant clam and the soaring eagle.

Think of a single web site as being a giant clam at the bottom of the ocean. Being bound to a defined location it simply opens it mouth and waits for its food to float in confident in the knowledge that the vast ocean will provide for its needs. When you only have a single web site to manage, the task is a relatively easy one. Certainly you can look at Search Engine Optimization (SEO) or paying to be a sponsored site on Google to try and "influence tides" in an effort to boost hits. You can even establish reciprocal link relationships with other similar sites, but in the end you are still confined to the "proverbial bottom of the ocean locale" which is your lone URL address.

Conversely, the eagle has to fight to survive through the growth process, but as a result of the hard work will ultimately soar high above the world below gaining a panoramic vision (and reach) that extends far beyond its nest.

The Syndicated Network Concept is very much like the eagle in that it requires considerably more work than managing a single web site.

As indicated earlier in this chapter, The PI Social Media Network includes the PI Window on Business Show on Blog Talk Radio, the Procurement Insights and PI Window on Business Blogs and the soon to be launched PI Inquisitive Eye and TV2 Young Entrepreneurs TV Channels.

The amount of work it takes to create these different venues within your personal network is considerably greater than having to create a single web site or blog. However, once these multiple venues are established it doesn't take as long as you might think to manage your network and position each site to feed content to sites other than your own. Using the Gladwell virus analogy you would think of your personal syndicated network as your classroom, with your fellow classmates representing the other sites such as Facebook, LinkedIn, and Twitter etc.

Now, let's take a moment to look at where we are from a logistics perspective in terms of interacting within the classroom framework using the PI model as the reference point.

When I schedule a show to air on the Blog Talk Radio site it takes me a few minutes to copy and format the show overview to both blogs. The first ripple!

Once posted to the blogs, I then use book marking tools such as OnlyWire which at the click of a button automatically distributes the posts regarding the show to all my social network contacts on LinkedIn, Facebook, and Twitter. When the connections that I have established within each social network or site in turn distributes the show information they received from me, this represents the second ripple. Using our Gladwell virus analogy, this is the same as your fellow classmates going out into the school yard during a break to interact and share information with students from other classes.

When your classmates and the students from the other classes with whom they have been in contact go home at the end of the day and share the information with their family and neighbours this is the third ripple. In the world of social networking these represent your secondary and tertiary level contacts.

Now you might wonder why I would have two different blogs disseminating the same information within the same "classroom." Isn't one sufficient? As I had indicated, while each blog does from time-to-time share or post the same information, both have a different look and feel with a fair amount of the content remaining unique to the respective audiences or readership. This means that one blog will usually appeal to one set of classmates, while the other will appeal to a different set of classmates. The great benefit of course is that all PI Social Media sites have varying degrees of interconnect ability which means that there is a cross-pollination element that will enable the reader or listener to move seamlessly between multiple PI Social Media Network venues.

Allow me to illustrate with the following example.

Through the Procurement Insights blog I have covered the Commonwealth of Virginia's eVA procurement platform since 2007.

As a result of a series of posts I had written the blog gradually built up a steady Virginia-based following. However, it was not until 2009 when I did a two-part segment on the PI Window on Business Show that the Commonwealth sent an e-mail blast to their 41,000 suppliers suggesting that they tune in to the broadcasts. In conjunction with the e-mail blast, Virginia also established a page on their eVA web site dedicated to my coverage of the Commonwealth's procurement practices and policies.

Without the PI Window on Business Show there would not have been the promotion to 41,000 individual businesses, or a page set-up linking the Commonwealth's visitors to my Main Show Page on the BTR web site. A page by the way that provides direct links to the Show's other on-demand broadcasts and corresponding blogs.

Are you beginning to see how relational or conversational marketing through the Syndicated Network Concept works . . . especially when someone else is spreading the word about your show?

In the case of the Virginia web site, the Commonwealth of Virginia has thousands if not tens of thousands of visitors each month. Of those, how many do you think will be drawn to visit a page under the heading "Articles on eVA by internationally acclaimed Procurement Expert." When they go to that site, how many will hit the link to listen to one or both of the PI Window on Business broadcasts?

This is the power of the Syndicated Network Concept. Now let's expand this model to increase your reach even further.

One of the main differences between elementary school and high school in terms of learning format is that with the former you take all of your classes in the same room with the same group of students. When you graduate to high school, you start each day with the same students in your home room. However, throughout the day you move to new classrooms for different subjects and in each classroom you are usually interacting with an entirely different group of students. This is the framework for the second stage in the Syndicated Network Concept.

Just today I wrote an article that I had posted to the Procurement Insights Blog. It was an interesting article (as I hope they all are) in that it dealt with the recent FTC decision to hold bloggers accountable for what they write.

Following the process outlined in the previous pages I also posted the article to the PI Window on Business Blog. From there I used the bookmarks to distribute the posts to my connections on Facebook, LinkedIn and Twitter (close to 10,000 direct contacts total). (Note: I had hosted a guest panel show on the PI Window on Business on the FTC subject five months earlier and therefore provided links to the on-demand player in both the Procurement Insights and PI Window on Business blog posts. In the context of the current day developments this stimulated listener interest. We will cover what I refer to as

Perpetual Promotion in the book's final chapter, but I wanted to introduce the concept here as the on-demand playback feature is one of the unique benefits of Blog Talk Radio as well as other leading social media platforms.)

I also have a sizable network on Ecademy which does not have a link established through the OpenWire service. Ecademy does however provide each member with a personal blog on their network.

I simply copied the article from the Procurement Insights Blog and posted it on my blog on Ecademy with the corresponding link to the on-demand version of the PI Window on Business Show that had aired five months earlier. It is important to note that I was not concerned with the fact that Ecademy readers could access the article outside of the Procurement Insights blog. What was important is that they had access that might otherwise not have been available to both the article and the corresponding show link.

An added advantage of the Ecademy blog is that the site also provides me with an OnlyWire-type capability to further distribute the post to other social networks including individual groups and clubs.

Given the expanded reach gained by not limiting myself to a one site mentality I have also duplicated this very same process through other similar-type platforms including knowledge resource sites such as EvanCarmichael.com where as a Platinum level contributing author my articles gain an additional 5,000 reads per month.

In addition to the above venues, the Procurement Insights Blog is also picked-up automatically by other publications through RSS feeds.

The point here is that the heavy lifting, which is creating quality content in the form of an article or show, requires the same amount of work whether you are posting to a single blog or through a Syndicated Network.

As illustrated by the Virginia example forcing the audience to a single site means that you will be missing a tremendous opportunity to extend your collaborative reach and drive the cross-pollination of readers, listeners and viewers across both your personal as well as extended network.

To sum it up, creating access points to diverse yet inter-related subject matter through multiple venues like the Procurement Insights and PI Window on Business Blogs, Internet radio on Blog Talk Radio and TV Channels on USTREAM, Blog TV and ooVoo means that your collective audience will grow rapidly over a relatively short period of time. An accomplishment that is virtually impossible through a traditional broadcast model in which you attempt to force the market to look at a single site or "stage."

Now that we have laid the framework for establishing your own Syndicated Network, let's spend some time on creating quality content relative to delivering an effective and powerful message that will pique interest and stir passions and of course increase listeners.

When you schedule a particular segment on Blog Talk Radio, and click on the submit button the platform automatically sends a message regarding the show to both Twitter and Facebook telling your network that they should tune in on the listed date and time.

The next step is to copy the show description and post to your blogs following the process outlined on the previous pages.

At this point I would like to suggest that you look at introducing video as a vehicle to promote both your upcoming as well as past segments.

While there are many sites through which you can create a video, the one I use almost exclusively is One True Media. It is a free service, although you will want to pay the nominal $4 per month to gain access to the premium features which includes incredible effects and music.

What is amazing about a video is that it enables you to expand your syndicated reach to networks such as YouTube, while simultaneously adding a dynamic and entertaining visual element to your blog posts.

When I first started creating videos to promote the PI Window on Business Show, I used to do one for each episode. Given time considerations, I have more recently started to prepare a single video providing the highlights for the upcoming month's entire schedule. I still create single segment videos for specials such as the 90-Minute Buy American guest panel discussion which also included an interview with Canada's Trade Minister.

Regardless of what you ultimately decide to do relative to frequency, creating a video is in and of itself a fun experience, and One True Media's easy to use functionality gives you the ability to produce a finished product on the same level as a top notch studio.

Another important element to effective promotion both pre-and post air date are guest bios and pictures (including links to books they have authored). While I will spend more time on post show marketing activities in Chapter 10, including the development of the Author Profile Page, and Featured Segment section, providing your audience base with information about your guests helps to establish a more personal link. To get a few ideas regarding the format of guest articles or posts visit the PI Window on Business Blog (http://piwindowonbusiness.wordpress.com/).

Finally, if you believe you have an interesting guest discussing an equally compelling topic, be sure to submit a request to have your segment featured through the "Feature my show" option in your personal account area on the Blog Talk Radio web site.

If selected by the station's editors, your show information including images will be featured in the "Today's Pick" and/or "Weekly Best" show box on the right hand index of the BTR web site.

There are many benefits associated with being featured including the opportunity to draw broadcast day traffic from Blog Talk Radio's 4.5 million monthly listener base, to using the featured segment(s) as a reference point for prospective guests and sponsors. We will discuss adding sponsors in greater detail in Chapter 10.

As you look back over the pages of this chapter I hope that you have gained a good understanding of the Syndicated Network Concept and how you can "arrange" complimentary yet individual media venues to establish an extended audience reach through conversational marketing.

# Chapter 7 - The "Virtual" Green Room

*"A central cohesive element . . . Something that holds the various elements together . . ."*

*Dictionary.com*

We are all of course familiar with the term linchpin. In fact I had first made reference to the term in the second chapter (page 17) relating to the importance of identifying the subjects that "stir" within you "the greatest levels of interest and emotion."

While some believe it to be named after Nathaniel Lynch, the "English mechanic who first patented its use in 1727," the small fastener that was used to "prevent a wheel or other rotating part from sliding off the axle," it is now used as a figure of speech to symbolize the "central cohesive element" holding together "various elements of a complicated structure."

In the case of hosting a Blog Talk Radio Show I would be hard pressed to find a better symbol for what I call the "Virtual" Green Room.

Even though this chapter is probably going to be one the shortest chapters in the history of book publishing, like its symbolic reference to the linchpin, do not mistake its size as a measure of the Virtual Green Room's importance to the success of your show.

Right about now, and likely having a general idea of that to which I am referring, you are still probably asking yourself what is a Virtual Green Room, and why is it so important?

In its most basic definition, it is the 10 to 15 minutes prior to air-time that the host and guest or guests come together through the switchboard to talk and make sure that the lines are working. (Note: as outlined in Chapter 3 pages 52, 53 – Example C, I ask all guests to call-in at least 10 minutes prior to air-time to ensure that if we encounter any technical difficulties with connecting through the main BTR switchboard in New York, this will provide us with an opportunity to rectify the problem in an orderly and timely fashion before going live. I also request that guests have access to their e-mail both prior to the start of the show as well during the broadcast itself. This ensures that I will be able to reach them and bring them back on-line quickly and easily should an interruption occur.)

In the traditional sense, and according to World Wide Words' Michael Quinion, "the term "Green Room" applies as much — if not more often — to the reception room in a television studio where guests wait before appearing." However, waiting is the last thing that I think about regarding the Green Room, virtual or otherwise.

As is the case prior to exercising, one is instructed to warm-up. The Virtual Green Room should also be viewed as an opportunity to warm-up before going on air. Specifically, and after the opening pleasantries, I like to engage my guests by discussing some of the highlights of the subject matter we will be covering during the broadcast. In essence, the interview for all intents and purposes starts before the eloquent BTR lady with the proper British accent makes the announcement "your show will go live in 5 seconds."

I personally believe that there are many benefits to Virtual Green Room discussions that make it the most important 10 to 15 minutes of each and every show.

The most obvious is that when the show actually begins you are not starting cold, but in fact are merely continuing a discussion that has already begun. This removes any pre-show butterflies – especially for guests (and yes, we all with varying degrees feel that pang of nervousness no matter how long we have been doing live interviews on either side of the mike).

I think it is the anticipation, or what I refer to as the pre-podium jitters that waiting in relative silence magnifies as it gives the guest an opportunity to think about what might or will be said, and how they will respond. As we all know a true discussion is not one of a planned or carefully measured tit-for-tat exchange, but is instead one of dynamic engagement where knowledge, experience and mutual interests converge in a spontaneous dialogue of fact, feeling and opinion. What I am talking about is hitting the show running at full steam through an actual discussion versus an anticipated one.

Without becoming too finite relative to speech patterns, in the time leading up to the show you are also given an opportunity to establish rapport timing. In other words you can synchronize the dialogue based on the fact that some guests prefer to pause for a few seconds or longer after a question is asked. Others may start talking the moment the last word of your sentence has been spoken. If you are talking with someone who has an accent or, English is their second language, you can hone in their unique speaking style and attune yourself to their manner of communicating.

The Virtual Green Room also provides an opportunity to address any last minute questions or concerns on the part of a guest, such as a previously unanticipated time restriction, or clarification on one of the questions.

If you are talking with a guest for whom this is the first time they have been on Blog Talk Radio, you are also afforded an opportunity to review the show's format with them including what happens after the theme music.

Of course ending where we began, the time before your show goes live provides you with an ability to address any unexpected technical problems. It is part of your state of proactive preparedness.

I can remember one incident in particular, which occurred just prior to the start of my first 90-Minute Special "The Pandemic Effect" at the end of May 2009.

After signing-on 15 minutes before air time I monitored the switchboard waiting for my guest's number to appear. Joining me on the show was a top researcher from the University of Minnesota's Center for Infectious Disease and Research Policy. Besides the fact that he was a leading authority on the impact of a pandemic on the nation's coal supply (and supply chains in general), he was my only guest for the first 60 minutes.

In short, if there was a problem, I was on my own. (Note: this is another reason why a back-up segment centered around you as the host is important as I can think of no worse last-minute ponderance than "what am I going to do if I am the only one on the show today?" You can also upload a recorded version of a previous show to serve as an emergency replacement, so have one uploaded and ready to go at the click of your mouse.)

As the 10 minute mark came and went, I quickly sent an e-mail to the individual indicating that we were 10 minutes from going live and to see if he was encountering any challenges with dialling-in.

Remember the emphasis I placed on asking all guests to maintain access to their e-mails?

Within a minute of my e-mail prompt being sent, the guest responded by return e-mail telling me that each time he had attempted to call-in, the system hung up on him. We are now at the 8-minute mark, and I can tell you that it pays to familiarize yourself with the BTR system through their brief but highly effective on-line video or "screencast" tutorials.

Knowing that it would only require a couple of minutes to close the switchboard and sign-off and then sign-on again, I instructed the guest to wait a couple of minutes while I rebooted the "system" and then try calling once more.

That's what I did, and with about a minute or two to spare we were ready when the show went live. Now even though we did not have the opportunity for an interview warm-up, the show was able to establish a rhythm relatively quickly partly assisted by the fact that the week before we had a somewhat lengthy pre-show interview.

This of course re-emphasizes the importance of proper preparation, which creates a track or touchstone that can be used to get back on course no matter what happens.

You can now see why I consider the Virtual Green Room to be the main linchpin of the entire show as it ultimately sets the tone as the final and most important check point leading into the live broadcast itself.

# Chapter 8 - Show Time! (Your Show Will Go Live in 5 Seconds)

*"Overture, curtains, lights . . . This is it, the night of nights . . . No more rehearsing and nursing a part . . . We know every part by heart"*

*Theme from the Bugs Bunny Show*

Remember my earlier references to the fact that "the easier it looks to do a show, the greater the effort in the behind the scenes planning and preparation?"

I then went on to ask the question, "So what is planning and preparation?"

Hopefully the previous seven chapters have provided both a clear answer as well as illustrating why preparation is the most important part of being a host on Blog Talk Radio (or for that matter Internet radio in general).

Think of it in the same way as planning a family vacation where you identify the destination, and then clearly outline the route you will take to arrive there safely and on time.

I also hope that I have shown you how to make the journey itself interesting and enjoyable from the standpoint of integrating the subjects about which you are most passionate, with both the hot topics of the day and the ready availability of the thought leaders to be interviewed.

So here we are . . . all dressed up and ready to go. Now what?

With the track properly laid, your primary focus can now shift to the show itself and in particular the conversational aspect of the interview.

Once again, the interview is not an adroit exchange of questions and answers, but should be viewed in the same light as a spirited discussion with a good friend over coffee at the local coffee house. In fact this is what I tell my guests prior to going live.

Think of our conversation as if we are sitting at a table sharing coffee and ideas on a subject with which we are both passionate. The people sitting at the surrounding tables are the audience to whom we have willingly given permission to eavesdrop on our lively exchange. The audience is certainly present, listening in because they too have an interest in what is being discussed. But they are not the focal point. In fact, what would happen if we were physically in a café and during our conversation we stopped talking, and paused to turn our attention to someone sitting at another table who had been listening in? How would they react when we looked at them? How would you respond if you were eavesdropping on a conversation? You would likely turn away immediately and look in another direction.

While I am of course not suggesting that an uninvited intrusion into a private conversation is acceptable, however with your Blog Talk Radio show eavesdropping is not only encouraged through a public broadcast, it is very much hoped for and welcomed.

In other words, be mindful of the listening audience, but not distracted by them.

This leads to a number of questions regarding listener or audience participation, including how to utilize the various advanced features afforded a Blog Talk Radio host such as the call-in and live Chat Room capabilities.

Let's start with the live, on-line Chat Room.

Like reading the operator's manual for your new car before taking it for a spin (you do read the manual first . . . right?), I would strongly suggest that you spend some time familiarizing yourself with the Chat Room's many features through the on-line BTR video "screencast" tutorial.

The Chat Room can be a veritable hub of activity during your discussion with your guest or guests, the simultaneous management of which becomes easier with time. The greatest benefit of the Chat Room is that it provides a venue for those who are not inclined to call-in to ask their question on-air.

While many listeners are still getting used to the interactive nature of a Blog Talk Radio, which means that you may have only one or two in the "room" during a segment, I have had as many as 19 or 20 at one time with at least 5 or 6 Chat Room visitors interacting with me, and each other.

Just after signing-on through the Host Dial-In number, I immediately activate the Chat Room from the main switchboard. Depending on your Internet link it usually takes a few seconds for the room to appear in a separate screen or browser window.

While you have the option of creating and saving a welcome message that can be used from the pull down icon right above your text entry screen, I like to type in a new message welcoming listeners to the show and providing them with additional information including links. I also post an initial question centered on the segment's theme that appears when they sign-in to listen.

Once again, and it will take a little practice, being able to simultaneously manage the Chat Room and interview provides a tremendous opportunity to solicit listener participation and feedback off-air during the broadcast. The fact that you have prepared a show outline in advance will make this task far easier to do because you will always have that important touchstone to keep you (or get you) back on track.

That said be sure to check Appendix B at the end of the book for specific links to what Blog Talk Radio refers to as "screencast tutorials" for all of the features of the Chat Room that are at your disposal.

Are you ready for accepting callers? Regardless of whether you are utilizing the Free Blog Talk Radio service or one of the two Premium Pay service packages, as a host you have the option to entertain callers from the listening audience.

Again, and as this book is focused on the practical versus technical aspects of hosting a show, I cannot stress enough the importance of taking the time to familiarize yourself with all the features that are available to you as a host through the BTR web site.

Specifically, while I will touch on the periphery of functionality as it relates to the art of hosting, this book is by no means meant to serve as an instruction manual.

With this in mind there are a number of key differences between the switchboard for the Free versus Premium packages, starting with the most important which is the absence of a call screening room.

In the very first chapter on page 9 I related the following story:

*In the latter instance I can recall tuning into another show where the exchange between a listener and guest disintegrated into a hostile exchange based on personal character versus the subject itself. This is hardly the atmosphere which creates an open and sharing environment. Even though the guest was obviously experienced at being interviewed, it irreversibly changed the tempo of the broadcast as the individual's guard was up for the remainder of the program. Nor would I imagine that any potential future guests listening into that broadcast would be eager to expose themselves to the possibility of a similar experience.*

With the Free or let's call it the standard switchboard, the only way to receive audience call-ins is to actually bring the caller on-air with nothing more that a displayed number. (Note: Even with the ability to screen calls under the Premium service, BTR does not recommend using the screening room feature unless a different individual other than the host – such as a producer, is managing that feature.)

Without the ability to screen callers prior to bringing them on-air you can of course run into the above referenced scenario, or risk having a non-intended caller situation where the number of an audience member who is just calling in to listen appears on your switchboard.

In the former situation, your skills as a host have to kick-in with you intervening to restore a respectful order to the broadcast. While you do not want capriciously and arbitrarily disconnect a listener who is expressing an honest difference of opinion with your guest, or for that matter yourself, there is a certain decorum to which all participants need to adhere. This includes no personal attacks, profanity, overt hostility or someone who is being disagreeable for the sake of being disagreeable.

If as a host you maintain an open and fair environment where the exchange of ideas are encouraged and shared in an atmosphere of mutual respect, even a disagreement can add much needed insight to a particular discussion or topic. In fact as Kenneth Boa wrote in his article titled Conflict Management, "conflict is a part of life."

Boa went on to write, "There is simply no getting away from this fact. As a leader, as a human being, you can be sure that you'll face relational conflicts. No leadership (or host) model exists that will totally eliminate disagreements or clashes of personality. In fact, the tension that comes from conflict can be healthy and beneficial to growth if dealt with correctly." This is exactly the kind of atmosphere it is incumbent upon you as a host to establish and maintain, one where there is a "healthy and beneficial growth" through either increased awareness, understanding or both.

One way for Free service hosts to possibly screen calls is through the Chat Room. Specifically, you indicate on all program related information and sites such as your show's blog and of course in the Chat Room itself, that all callers must indicate their interest to talk on-air and provide their name, number and of course the nature of their question and/or comment. Without providing you with this information via the Chat Room, you will not be able to "welcome" them to participate in the live discussion with your guest or guests.

The non-intended caller scenario is certainly less dramatic, although I liken it to the character Ben Stein played in the movie Ferris Beullers Day Off. I am sure you remember the somewhat nasally "monotone voice" teacher doing the morning attendance calling the name Beuller, Beuller?

In the non-intended caller situation, and upon deactivating the mute button beside the displayed number, the host invariably (and unintentionally) does a Stein imitation having to repeat the phrase, hello caller . . . hello is anybody there . . . is anybody there.

Having to do this refrain once isn't so bad, but by the time you get to the fourth or fifth number you have used up enough recording time to warrant an edit.

Alternatively, with the advanced features of the new switchboard available to Premium subscribers, the host can focus his attention on the on-air activities, while a second person (producer or whatever title you deem appropriate) brings callers into the off-air screening room. The advantage here is that even the non-intended callers who may be somewhat hesitant about speaking on air, will likely feel more comfortable within the confines of the virtual screening room to let the producer know that they are just listening in through their phone line.

For those who are eager to share their thoughts with the host and guest or guests on-air, the screening room feature enables the producer to get the name of the caller as well as their purpose for wanting to become part of the live conversation.

This information is entered by the producer, and is available to the host simply by passing their mouse over the Caller Info icon beside the caller's number. While there is no guarantee that an unwanted caller will not get through occasionally, it is less likely to occur especially if the screening standards are properly set and adhered to by the individual manning the switchboard.

Beyond the Chat Room and the switchboard, always be mindful of the clock.

In the upper right hand corner of your switchboard (above the call-in numbers) is a real time clock which tells you how many minutes are left in your show.

When I first began doing interviews, it was almost a given that I would run overtime. This meant that the live or streaming broadcast would end, and the interview would continue off-air. This was not a problem as the show is recorded and made available on an on-demand basis in its entirety shortly after the broadcast ends. However, the live audience would miss out on the remainder of the conversation, and then be forced to listen to the on-demand version to hear the balance of the program. While the on-demand version is accessible at the convenience of the listener, the general feeling on the part of the audience is that if I am already tuned in, I would like to get the whole story then and there rather than having to come back.

As Free service hosts can record up to 2 hours and Premium service hosts up to 3 hours, it is not a question of having enough time through BTR, but is instead a question of effective time management.

For me, the resolution was to ultimately increase my shows to 60 minutes in length and make a firm commitment that the one-hour mark represented a hard stop. I then monitored where I was in the show's outline by different time points, starting at the 30-minute mark. Based on where I was in the interview, I could then gauge how much time was needed to ask the important questions listed in my show outline.

Now it should be noted that the number of questions I ask during the live broadcast are usually less than the total number of questions I had originally provided to the guest(s). So when I talk about effective on-air time management, I am not suggesting that the goal is to make certain that you ask every question. Nor am I endorsing a long-winded meandering show that digresses into any number of unplanned detours.

What I am saying is that the questions you actually use are dependent upon the nature or flow of the conversation itself, while still adhering to the format to ensure that the promised insights are ultimately delivered to the listening audience.

For example, you do not want to cut short an interesting response from your guest, or shy away from delving deeper into an interesting comment because you have to "rush" to ask all of your questions. These are natural extensions of the main theme through which the greatest insights and ideas are usually delivered. The key is to make certain that you are mindful of the particular segment or theme around which the track (and related questions) are based, and be able to progress within that framework toward the ultimate audience goal.

As you get down to the final 4 or 5 minutes of the broadcast, it is always a good idea to let both the guest(s) and audience know that you are in the last few minutes of the program and that you would like to ask one or two final questions. You can also ask the guest(s) if they would like to wrap-up with a few final thoughts on the subject matter being discussed.

Unlike the beginning of your show, the closing theme music does not automatically kick-in. You have to manually select the play option button from the "Files" Section of your switchboard which is between the "Show Information" and "Switchboard" Sections.

I would suggest that you have both a 30 and 60-second version of the theme music available, using the 30-second at the show's start and the 60-second for the show's conclusion. (Note: Referencing page 97 from the previous chapter, the theme music is in the same section where your uploaded recording of a previous broadcast can be accessed in the event that you have to pre-empt an originally scheduled program. As is the case with any uploaded file, be sure to chose the right one because once you hit the play button, there is no way to stop the recording.)

Relating to sound quality, I have usually found that hosting through your landline usually produces the best quality sound on a consistent basis. That said the option to host the show through Skype using your headset has had mixed reviews from a quality standpoint, but quite frankly it is still an extremely viable option for many reasons.

To begin neither you nor your guests, incur long distance charges when Skype is used. While you can obviously use a headset for your phone, I like using the headset with my computer as it keeps everything to do with your broadcast at your fingertips through your keyboard.

Regarding the headset itself, expense does not translate into superior sound quality. I originally went with a moderately expensive brand name headset only to stop after one broadcast as the sound was poor when I listened to the on-demand playback. Today I use a no name headset that cost less than $5 and the sound is far better.

Now I am not suggesting that everyone should go out and purchase the cheapest headset they can find, because ultimate sound quality is influenced by any number of factors including your system, software being used etc. What I am saying is that your decision regarding equipment should be based on consistent sound quality performance. (Note:

You can improve sound quality by adjusting the volume settings in Skype whereby a lower setting will usually remove a certain level of distortion.)

For these reasons, I would at least try both the phone and the Skype option and gauge the sound quality of the on-demand broadcast.

One final recommendation is that immediately following the show, and obviously once you are off the air, be sure to contact your guest or guests by phone if possible (otherwise e-mail), to thank them for joining you and obtain their feedback on their Blog Talk Radio experience. I will be expanding on how you can use this feedback to help you to improve the overall quality of your show in the next chapter "Reviewing the Game Film." However the fact that you take the time to give the courtesy call will be appreciated by most guests, some of whom will also ask you for your feedback on their performance.

This provides you with a tremendous opportunity to build a relationship with your guest that can lead to a return appearance or a reference point for future guests.

Beyond what has already been covered in this chapter, the most important recommendation I can make is to become part of the discussion and enjoy the opportunity to talk with interesting people who through your well-researched questions will add a unique perspective to the subject matter being covered.

# Chapter 9 - Reviewing the Game Film

*"In a game of enormous pressure and uncertainty, Dick Vermeil was determined to succeed as a head coach in the NFL by outworking everybody else. He would sell his players on the need to practice harder than they had ever practiced before. And he would outwork all of them by watching film until the middle of the night, then wiping his eyes clear and getting up for an 8:00 AM staff meeting."*

*From the book "Dick Vermeil: Whistle in His Mouth, Heart on His Sleeve"*

As you have probably already noted from the early chapters of this book, I am very much a sports fan. It is undoubtedly hard to miss when my very reminiscences of traditional radio are centered on broadcasts in which the *"fierce rivalry between hockey's giants the Montreal Canadians and Toronto Maple Leafs brought together four brothers (myself being the youngest), in which three cheered on the beloved blue and white against the hated Habs."*

My numerous references to sports however extend beyond an interest that has spanned four decades, as there are parallels between the preparation that goes into getting ready for a game, and the effort associated with putting on a quality show. We have of course covered what proper preparation entails in the previous chapters.

That said and similar to the preparation that goes into hosting a show on Blog Talk Radio, the post show analysis is equally important.

Picking-up where we left off in the previous chapter relative to calling every guest following each broadcast, understanding what worked well during the show, as well as where there is room for improvement enables you to progressively and proactively raise the level of your performance each time you hear the words "Your Show Will Go Live in 5 Seconds."

The importance of placing an immediate call to your guest or guests is that the just concluded on-air discussion is still fresh in everyone's mind, and therefore you will get a gut-level, first impression opinion that hasn't been filtered through the lens of pre-show expectation and post show reality. I generally find that this leads to some interesting insights that may not have likely been shared a day or two or for that matter even a few hours later.

Generally speaking, the post-show comments have by-and-large been extremely positive, so providing you with actual examples of how the show could have been improved from a personal standpoint might be a bit difficult. However, even consistently good reviews are an important indicator that you are on the right track.

The point is simply this, whether positive or negative, whatever the actual feedback you receive from your guests are important as these are the people with whom you had just shared the "audio spotlight." They are coming from a similar experience and therefore have the best vantage point by which to offer constructive input.

The next step in "reviewing the game film" is to access the specific segment's Show Page on the BTR web site to see who had tuned into the show.

Keeping in mind of course that the picture for only those individual listener's that have actually registered with BTR and have set-up a profile page will appear in your segment's Show Page. Regardless of how many pictures are displayed, I make it a point to click on each one and send them the following note under the heading "Thank you for tuning in to . . . PI Window on Business:"

*Thank you for taking the time out of your busy schedule to join us on the PI Window on Business Show. I hope that you found our program to be informative as well as entertaining.*

*We look forward to your joining us again in the future. In the meantime to learn more about today's guests as well as other show information visit the PI Window on Business Blog at http://piwindowonbusiness.wordpress.com/*

*Best Regards,*

*Jon Hansen*

*Host, PI Window on Business Show*

This provides you with the first opportunity to connect directly with the listening audience to determine if the objective of the program, i.e. impart insight, create awareness, generate discussion etc. has actually been achieved. It also provides you with an opportunity to build your BTR connections, as a good percentage of the "registered" listeners will be other hosts.

On the subject of fellow BTR hosts, I would like to ever so briefly touch on the importance of having other hosts tuning in to your show. To begin, and as indicated in the first chapter, it is important to remember that there is a general absence of competitiveness between hosts. In essence, shows do not compete against one another as do the networks in the world of television. Because of this, building a useful and collaborative presence within the BTR community provides many benefits, including the fact that you are likely to receive some of the most interesting and useful comments from someone who is your contemporary.

After all, an individual who has hosted 50, 100 or more shows can provide you with a perspective based on their own experiences that can save you both time and the frustration of having to learn by trial and error. This includes how to fully utilize the BTR platform, or how you can most effectively avoid and/or respond to the technical difficulties that do come up from time-to-time.

There are of course cross marketing opportunities, a topic about which I will cover in greater detail in the last chapter "Perpetual Promotion."

Getting back to obtaining listener feedback as part of the review process, outside of the BTR community you will also want to engage your connections within the various social networking groups to which you are a member.

Given my references to the importance of groups in multiple areas including information gathering for segment ideas (page 18), identifying and connecting with possible guests (page 22), general marketing of the show (page 54), and of course pre-show or segment promotion (page 82), it should come as no surprise that groups offer the ideal venue through which to solicit listener feedback.

I personally belong to 43 different groups on LinkedIn. While some share similar areas of interest and focus such as procurement, government policy, emerging social media to name only a few, I can think of no better way to connect with listeners outside of the actual broadcast itself.

One such example is a segment that aired on April 23rd titled "Unemployed Excellence - Why Lean, Six Sigma Have Left Some People Out in the Cold."

Featuring an interview with critically acclaimed author and Lean, Six Sigma expert Forrest Breyfogle III (who is the creator of the Integrated Enterprise Excellence process), the show has had close to 1,100 listeners. I was pleased with this result given that is was only my fifth show, and that the subject matter was focused on enterprise operations, which is hardly going to land you on the front page of the local paper.

Following the exact process that I have outlined throughout the book, I immediately posted the link to the on-demand segment on a number of Six Sigma related LinkedIn groups asking the question "Do you agree with the points raised in today's show, "Unemployed Excellence - Why Lean, Six Sigma Have Left Some People Out in the Cold?"

The first indication that the show hit home with the listeners was the fact that between 20 to 30 people took the time to write in. Of these, the majority agreed with the points raised and even those who didn't, still felt that is was a good show.

Looking back, I realize that the response was ultimately more important than it was at the time it happened because it provided the level of listener "echo" which tells you that you are going in the right direction relative to sharing useful insights.

As the above process is repeated, your collective conversational reach grows exponentially and with it the opportunity to interview terrific guests regarding timely topics, that in turn generates increased awareness and interest. This is what ultimately led Blog Talk Radio to make me a featured host across their network, as well as on-air acknowledgements from the likes of bestselling author Shel Israel who during the September 10th, 2009 broadcast stated that "according to his research, I have one of the most popular (BTR) shows in North America."

Going beyond the immediate efforts of calling guests following the show, sending thank you for tuning in notes to registered listeners and soliciting feedback through the various social networking groups, establishing a permanent and on-going rapport with listeners is critical as it enables you to turn a one-time listener into a regular follower.

The best and most effective way of doing this is through the creation of a blog.

As you may recall from the second chapter (page 29), I made the statement that "through both unilateral as well as reciprocal syndication the PI Social Media Network can reach between 1 and 1.3 million people each month." My blogs were, and continue to be a key factor in achieving this conversational reach. In particular, the PI Window on Business Blog has become the seamless bridge that links post show activities to pre-show promotion in a single perpetual cycle of engagement.

In fact, the PI Window on Business Blog serves multiple purposes from providing information on upcoming segments and guest profiles, to breaking news stories on hot topics involving the world of social media to interesting and even thought-provoking commentary. Let's not forget about the multi-media experiences including videos and of course the direct access readers' gain to the growing library of past PI Window on Business broadcasts to listen to at their own convenience on an on-demand basis.

The collective value of the blog's ready availability is that it enables me to connect with the show's audience thereby establishing an accessible brand of reliability, trust and quality. It is in fact our Mission Statement, calling card and discussion facilitator all-in-one.

This escalating level of engagement that begins the moment your show ends is very much similar in concept to what Jim Collins referred to in his book Good to Great as "The Flywheel" concept.

Referencing an excerpt from his book Collins stated that "There was no single defining action, no grand program, no one killer innovation, no solitary lucky break, no miracle moment. Rather, the process resembled relentlessly pushing a giant heavy flywheel in one direction, turn upon turn, building momentum until a point of breakthrough, and beyond."

This is what I have been talking about in both this chapter as well as the entire book itself. It requires a constant and persevering effort to successfully build, and maintain a quality show on Blog Talk Radio. I am not, as indicated in the first chapter (pages 11 and 12) "highlighting the importance of advanced preparation" and the overall commitment that is required, to dissuade you from "taking on the responsibility of hosting a show on BTR." It is my personal belief that while there is a great deal of effort required, if you are doing what you love you will never have to work another day in your life.

However, this contemplation of effort does provide us with the perfect place in which to take a reflective pause before we move on to the 10th and final chapter, "Perpetual Promotion."

Of course promotional activities are for many the most enjoyable undertaking, from making videos using on-line tools such as One True Media, to creating sound bites and news flashes with what has become known as "The Audio Twitter," Cinch (which is another great Blog Talk Radio social network – networking tool), and of course leveraging the various social media networks and services to get the message out about your show.

That said I deliberately chose to end the book with the perpetual promotion theme as marketing and promotional activities are often at the top of the "to do" list. This is understandable because it is fun to do. Create a buzz to start a wave of interest. Then once the interest is peaked, and we know that demand (or audience) is there we can work out the details of the show. Just let me get out in front of a mike and we will go from there.

By the way, there is nothing wrong with just grabbing the mike and reaching out to friends, family and the unknown masses. My brother-in-law and his uncle from the east coast in Canada often considered starting a show and just talking about whatever hit their fancy on that particular day. Ex military men they undoubtedly would have more than a few interesting points of view to share.

I am certain that even under those casual conditions certain parts of this book will prove to be quite useful, and therefore I would encourage you to pick and chose those things which fit within your interest's framework.

However, if you are looking to do a show in which you want to build a sustained following, in which you interview guests who are at the top of their game, then the order of activities will be important to ensure a well established program track has been laid down.

In short why expend energy on promoting a show in which the unanticipated amount of work to produce a quality program means that you are going to either stop broadcasting or, broadcast only occasionally.

This is the reason why I start with creating a quality show first and marketing second.

If after these first nine chapters you still feel strong about hosting a regularly scheduled show then embrace the vehicles and tools that I will be covering in the upcoming chapter with all alacrity.

Conversely, and if after reading the first couple of chapters you decide that an occasional on-air appearance will more that satiate your appetite for hosting a talk radio show, then enjoy and follow the suggestions in the next chapter in the context of simply having fun.

# Chapter 10 - Perpetual Promotion

*"In a freefalling economy, there is a certain comfort to be found in the Harry Potter perpetual promotion machine. Not only have the novels and their spin-offs — movies, DVDs, action figures, T-shirts, lunch boxes, earrings, desk sets and so on — earned billions for their creator, J.K. Rowling, but over the last 12 years, the franchise has helped pay the mortgages of untold numbers of publicists, store clerks, prop builders, toy factory workers and popcorn sellers."*

*From the CBC News article "Harry Potter and the Half-Blood Prince"*

Without a doubt, the Harry Potter franchise has been (and continues to be) one of the most proliferate promotion "machines" in history creating a global fan base and in the process reeling in record earnings.

The franchise's ultimate reach, according to the CBC News story, even impacts the everyday economy permeating all stations of life from publicists to popcorn sellers.

At the risk of sounding repetitive, which I will gladly do to make an important point, the multiple venues and products through which the Potter series has been promoted would have amounted to little if the core product – the J.K. Rowling books – were found wanting. In short, all of the ever increasing resources that have historically been confined to the domains of big publishers, advertising agencies, and creative production houses that are now within the hands of the individual through programs such as One True Media, USTREAM, StumbleUpon, an ever increasing number of social networks and even Blog Talk Radio itself would mean nothing if the quality of your core product re program does not consistently deliver value to the listening audience.

This again is why the first 9 chapters of "Your Show Will Go Live in 5 Seconds" was spent on creating an Internet Radio Program that engages, informs, empowers and yes even entertains. Once you have all of the key elements combined in a professional, people oriented show format, your "perpetual marketing" efforts will act as an incendiary spark that will ignite a fire within each listener that will leverage the viral nature of the social media world to build a sustainable buzz.

The tools or resources that I will be discussing will, for veritable pennies, provide the individual or small media enterprise with the capability to produce high-quality, professional marketing content that will be on a par with the majority of large traditional production houses.

Remaining true to the general format of this book, there will be a sequential logic to what tools are engaged and when, in a step-by-step process towards building the kind of marketing momentum that reflects the previously discussed Flywheel concept in Collins' Good to Great.

It will take time (but not as much as you would expect), and a good deal of initial or up-front heavy lifting, but once your perpetual marketing flywheel breaks through, it will take on a life and momentum of its own that will probably surprise you.

What will not surprise is that almost everything that has already been covered will be presented here within the context of a definitive action plan. Specifically, and this is the exciting part, as you progress through the pages of this final chapter of "Your Show Will Go Live in 5 Seconds," a series of light bulbs will begin going off like the photographers' cameras on Oscar Night or the opening kick-off for the Super Bowl.

The reason is quite simple, having understood the individual elements associated with creating a successful show, we will now show how the pieces seamlessly come together within a collective framework.

Just as we opened Chapter 5 with the famous Walt Disney quote "the best way to get started is to quit talking and begin doing," we will now review the practical steps towards creating your own Potter-esque perpetual marketing flywheel.

(Step 1) The Power of the Blog

Before we go any further, if you have not yet created a blog stop reading this book and go and create one. If you have one, but do not make at least 3 to 5 posts per week, you are only slightly ahead of someone who doesn't have a blog. In essence, you are also starting a square one.

A personal blog is the hub of your marketing wheel. It is your way of establishing your virtual personality and ultimately your brand and media franchise. It is that important.

While you can use a variety of platforms, with many diverse features including a self-hosted blog, the shortest distance from right here and now is found in the simplicity of services such as a Wordpress.com (the one with which I started and continue to use to this day).

Within a matter of a few minutes you can create your blog and then leveraging an ever expanding array of themed templates and related bells and whistles you can add the personal touches that reflect who you are and what you have to say.

When I launched the Procurement Insights Blog it was as stated earlier in this book, more an act of convenience rather than a means to developing my personal brand.

However, and as the amazing tools and services of the social media world became more readily available, I soon recognized that a blog is not merely an extension of traditional media such as newspapers and magazines, but instead represented a true paradigm shift in the way in which we communicate with one another.

To use the same analogy I had used in the forward of this book, think of a blog as if you are getting ready for that first date with the prettiest girl (or for the ladies, handsomest guy) in your school. How your blog looks, what it says in the colorful prose of your text will tell the reader who you are and what you have to offer.

Even after a successful first encounter, where you are fortunate enough to make a connection, it would be unlikely that for subsequent dates you would either show up late or not all . . . at least not if you wanted the relationship to continue. Make no mistake through your blog you are establishing a relationship with your readers.

This means that a sporadic post here and there or the posting of half-hearted content will only serve to frustrate and ultimately undermine your efforts to establish a sustained following.

This is why one of the very first things I highlighted as being important was to tap "into and coordinate" your personal passion for a subject "with those of your guests and audience without playing to individual interests alone." In other words you are not writing a blog to appeal or appease, but to engage, discuss and even debate those central issues that are most important to you and your readership.

There is an integrity of purpose and a sense of mission when you write about the things that are most important to you which comes through better than any well written text or sharply designed site. Readers can sense unctuous musings a mile away, and will avoid you like the proverbial plague. On the other hand when you open yourself up to them, making your self vulnerable in the process, people will be drawn to you like a bee to a flower or a bear to honey.

Given that this book is about hosting your own Blog Talk Radio show, it is also worth noting that readers can and will become listeners. It is a natural progression (and fair expectation) that if people are engaged by the articles of a writer, they will most certainly be interested in hearing what that same writer has to say over the virtual airwaves. For those of you who are baseball fans, a blog serves as a "farm system" for developing a future and ready made listener base.

Now, if you do not have a blog and are thus starting with a clean slate, then you will want to establish a consistent brand right out of the gate. This means that the look and feel of your blog, including its name should be aligned with that of your show.

While there will be areas or posts that will reflect the specific segments from the show itself, the blog affords you with an opportunity to expand on stories, highlight the key points from an on-air interview, as well as new insights.

The blog will also serve as an important show resource in that it will list past segments including guest profiles and links to the corresponding on-demand players. So even though there will be obvious and welcomed differences relative to content, there will still be a continuity that will extend rather than differentiate the brand between these different mediums.

If you already have a blog, the question that needs to be asked and answered right off the bat is simply this, have you dedicated the time and energy necessary to have developed even the basic foundation of a sustained following. In other words, if I stopped posting to my blog today, would anyone notice.

It seems like a funny question to ask as one would assume that depending on the length of time you have been writing to your blog, you would of at least have gained some insight through reader comments and even a rudimentary tracking of site visits that you have been talking to someone other than yourself.

The point of asking this question is to determine if you have anything that would warrant a continued effort in supporting the current blog, or if even a re-branding would be a worthwhile investment of your time and energy. You of course are the only one that can answer this, however if maintaining a blog with a marginal following detracts you from putting forth the necessary effort to build your show including the required dedication to maintaining a properly aligned branded blog, then I would drop the existing blog without any hesitation or question.

In my case, and as you already know, the Procurement Insights Blog was and still is the jewel in the PI Social Media Network's crown. This is not meant to take away anything from the PI Window on Business Show or Blog, nor the soon to be launched PI Inquisitive Eye and TV2 Young Entrepreneurs TV Channels (and associated blogs). It is just that the Procurement Insights Blog was that first important cornerstone from where the PI Window on Business Show and subsequent mediums originated. Like the first born in any family, there is a sense of enduring comfort and passion that continues to fuel the ideas and concepts that go into each and every Procurement Insights Blog post to this day. Procurement is after all part of my own professional history, and is one in which I remain firmly rooted.

With a syndicated readership reach of more than 300,000 each month worldwide, rebranding or discontinuing were not options. This is even truer today in that the functional silos of both private and public corporations, in which interest and focus was confined to a narrowly defined set of responsibilities or job duties have by and large started to come down. The result is that procurement professionals, who have always had diverse interests if not in their professional lives most certainly in their private lives, want to know more about the world around them. This includes the emergence and influence of social media and networking, expanded career path opportunities through leadership development concepts and of course purchasing's growing influence in what has become an increasingly complex global marketplace.

The best way to sum up the reasons why I continued with the Procurement Insights Blog after launching the PI Window on Business Show on Blog Talk Radio was best summed up by a fellow industry pundit, Charles Dominick from Next Level Purchasing.

In a July 17$^{th}$, 2009 post to his blog, Charles' Purchasing Certification Blog under the heading "Procurement Insights Expands its Reach" Charles wrote, "Procurement blogger extraordinaire Jon Hansen, who publishes the Procurement Insights blog, is getting a louder voice in cyberspace. His Internet-based talk radio show, PI Window on Business, has become a "Featured" program on Blog Talk Radio.

What does this mean?

It means that the live show, one of the only if not the only of its kind, will get front page exposure on the Web site of Blog Talk Radio - a growing portal for thousands of Internet talk shows that regularly include celebrity guests. So, on a broadcast day, procurement may be a featured topic right along side TV stars. Quite an accomplishment, if you think about it!"

Charles closed his post with the following comment "Congratulations go out to Jon for his good work in raising the profile of procurement, which benefits us all!"

If your current blog has this kind of following, then by all means continue with doing the things that has made it a noteworthy presence in the indigenous market it serves. You will of course still need to create a new blog that is directly linked to your Blog Talk Radio show. However, and having successfully established the first blog, it should not present too onerous a task to create and maintain the second. I actually maintain three blogs (the third is the Christian Blog "The Light of Love").

Alternatively, and if you find that you are already pressed for time as it is, if your original blog has failed to gain any meaningful traction, then with a final post to its readers indicate that you will be launching a new show, or already have a show on Blog Talk Radio, and that you will be establishing a new similarly branded blog. While you would like to encourage each one of your readers to follow you on the new blog, if they chose not to then thank them for the investment of their time and interest in the current blog, letting them know that this will be the final post.

Even though you will no longer be making an active contribution to the old blog, this farewell message will remain for anyone who does happen to visit the site. It is of course a classy way to close the chapter on one blog before opening the door on the new blog. Even if only a handful of people actually read it, it will stand out with them and may come back to benefit you in some unexpected way in the future. By the way, make certain that you have already created the new blog before publishing the farewell post as you will definitely want to provide a link to the new site.

(Step 2) Connecting With People and Events

So you have a blog, and you have a show. You are for all intents and purposes ready to go. Almost without fail, the very next questions that people usually ask is what do I write and talk about and, of even greater importance "do I have enough material to do more than one or two shows, or write one or two blog posts?"

It is not an entirely unreasonable question to ask. My own concerns were not centered on running out of topics to either write or talk about on air, that's the benefit of having written what was at the time close to 250 posts and in the processing realizing that there is always something happening that is worthy of attention. My concerns had more to do with filling the show's length.

As discussed in the $2^{nd}$ Chapter (page 27), it was the main reason why I chose to initially do a 30-minute segment. My thinking of course was tied to the fact that "I would rather have something worthwhile to say and run out of time, than have all the time in the world with nothing to say." At 30 minutes, I felt reasonably comfortable that I could fill the time slot with quality information that I had hoped would leave my audience with the feeling that they "always wanted a little bit more."

Well you know from this book as well as tuning into my show (you tune in on a regular basis . . . right?), we would have no problem filling 60 to 90 minutes let alone what turned out to be a paltry 30 minutes.

Sounds great, right? But I still haven't answered the questions relative to "what" as in the "what do I write or talk about," and the where in terms of "where do I go to get this information." After all, and depending on your individual experiences, material which can fill the pages of a blog post 3 or 4 times per week, let alone a 30-minute talk show can present a dissuasive obstacle.

But here is the good news, like the famous Seinfeld episode where George is admonished for double dipping, you in essence will learn to double dip in the bowl of social networking.

Social networks are an amazing phenomenon that ironical reflects the concept of social capital that was defined by L.J. Hanifan in 1916.

In an excerpt from my opening remarks in the June 4th broadcast "The Psychology of Social Networking," I referred to Hanifan's definition as well as the emergence of social networking as follows:

*"..That in life which tends to make these tangible substances count for most in the daily lives of people: namely good will, fellowship, sympathy, and social intercourse among the individuals and families who make up a social unit... The individual is helpless socially, if left to himself... If he comes into contact with his neighbor, and they with other neighbors, there will be accumulation of social capital, which may immediately satisfy his social needs and which may bear a social potentiality sufficient to the substantial improvement of living conditions in the whole community. The community as a whole will benefit by the cooperation of all its parts, while the individual will find in his associations the advantages of the help, the sympathy, and the fellowship of his neighbors."*

*A 2006 Forrester Report about social computing used the term "groundswell" to refer to "a spontaneous movement of people using online tools to connect, take charge of their own experience, and get what they need-information, support, ideas, products, and bargaining power–from each other."*

*This of course raises the question, is Hanifan's 1916 definition regarding social networking a reflection of its true intent that is best achieved or realized through a face-to-face interaction, or does our current technology driven mediums, while lacking in the realm of up front and personal contact, deliver greater business and social value to what has become a global community? This is "The Psychology of Social Networking."*

I shared this with you for a number of reasons including my belief that it is one of the best ways to present the "social nature" of social networking in the context of a common human experience that is not confined to a particular era or the development of an advanced technology. In short, social networking is meeting and engaging people with whom you can and often share similar interests.

Specifically, and while not being the only source of information, social networks are the ideal incubator for ideas, discussions and even the debate surrounding current day events. To be even more succinct, social networks and in particular the groups within each network are one of the most vibrant and therefore vital sources of the kind of material you require to write a blog post or produce and host a Blog Talk Radio program.

The double dipping analogy is linked to the fact that the very source of your writing inspiration or show theme is also one of the first venues through which you will post information on your show.

I will give you an example referencing the previous chapter, and in particular page 114 when I informed you that "I personally belong to 43 different groups on LinkedIn."

In that particular example I had talked about the April 23$^{rd}$ segment titled "Unemployed Excellence - Why Lean, Six Sigma Have Left Some People Out in the Cold." Based on a question that was posted in one of the Six Sigma groups on LinkedIn coupled with the subsequent flurry of responses I knew that there was something worth examining closer.

The pressing question (or trigger) was based on the fact that amongst the first to be laid off as a result of the financial crisis were those professionals who possessed the Six Sigma accreditation and expertise. This had a great many professionals including leading Six Sigma experts, educational institutions and past, present and potential students scratching their heads in literal bewilderment. It was an important topic, and yes it also had the makings for a great PI Window on Business segment.

As one of the Procurement Insights Blog's sponsors, Smarter Solutions and in particular its founder Forrest Breyfogle III was the obvious choice to tackle this subject.

Having written a highly successful series of books, some of which were used as text reference material in a number of educational institutions including Universities, Breyfogle would (and I am happy to say did), bring a level of expertise and perspective from multiple vantage points that provided invaluable insight for the listening audience. This is the first dip . . . identifying and extracting information.

The second dip was directly related to my providing the links to both the PI Window on Business blog posts and the link to the actual show itself on Blog Talk Radio.

Approximately 7 to 10 days prior the show's air date, I went into each of the Six Sigma related sites to which I belonged, and indicated that the PI Window on Business may very well have an answer to this terribly perplexing question. I followed the same track after the show's live air date by posing the question "Do you agree with the points raised in today's show, "Unemployed Excellence - Why Lean, Six Sigma Have Left Some People Out in the Cold?" with the corresponding link to the On-Demand replay.

Besides boosting what had been solid listening numbers for a subject that by its very nature is somewhat narrow in scope as compared to a Paris Hilton melodrama, the second dip or follow-up question produced between 20 and 30 reader responses. This established a higher profile within a number of the related groups, many of whom I am sure still tune in to the show today.

The key point that I am illustrating with the above example is that social networks and in particular the groups that operate within the framework of these social platforms are a replenishable information resource that literally tells you what the hot topics of the day are in your areas of expertise and interest. An added benefit – and again think of the double dipping analogy – is that the very same people who are driving an issue's importance are the very people you want to have has listeners.

If you are a medical professional, there are groups for this area of practice. A lawyer, botanist, musician or a graduate of USC, there is likely a group or a club on every social network through which you can join and exchange ideas. You can even create your own groups as I have done for the PI Window on Business Show on LinkedIn, Facebook, Ecademy, Perfect Networker and even a guest resource group on Reputation Network Inquisix.

The advantage with groups is that you can set-up your membership to automatically receive updates whether they are related to another member asking a question or sharing the link to a thought-provoking article through your personal e-mail account.

Now I feel that it is important to add that your view of, or interests in social networking groups cannot be solely tied to what you can get as a result of becoming a member. The true value in being part of a group is that you also have an opportunity to make a valuable contribution. This contribution can certainly take the form of scheduling a segment that would be of specific interest to your group or groups, the link to which can be shared with other group members through a "News" post. However, you can also add value by reading and responding directly to questions outside of the realms of your blog and show. What I am talking about is a balanced give and take relationship, starting with the giving on your part. If you approach group participation with this frame of mind, you will not only be pleased but also amazed at the opportunities that will suddenly present themselves to you.

There are of course numerous other venues through which you can gain insights into breaking stories or industry developments from traditional newspapers to RSS feeds of blogs you discover on the Internet to even a Wikipedia. My point is simply this, go to where the people are and you will have an inexhaustible resource of interesting subjects, listeners and even guests.

It just so happens that the place "to be" can be found quickly and easily within the ever expanding number of social networks. My own preferences have seen me use what I call a "nest and connect" strategy in which LinkedIn, Ecademy, Facebook and now Perfect Networker serve as primary "nesting" sites.

The "nest and connect" concept is based upon the premise that due to having a limited amount of time to develop their presence in a social network, each person has one or even two primary networks with which they spend most of their time. When they need to expand their reach outside of their primary network community they can do so through their sites' available APIs and associated links to connect with other networks on an as needed basis?

In relation to the focus of this book, and as suggested by individual group demographics you will want to check out all four of the networks to which I belong. You will also want to start using

Twitter as well as the new Audio Twitter which is Blog Talk Radio's Cinch.

Beyond that it is important that you become familiar with the various social networks and related outreach capabilities each posses as this will form a key part of creating awareness and driving audience numbers for your show. There are of course a variety of resources, some of which I have listed in Appendix C of this book.

One final word regarding social networks is to remind you that Blog Talk Radio is also a form of social network where you can build relationships with both hosts and registered listeners in much the same way that you would within any of the standard networks like a LinkedIn or Facebook. Be certain to familiarize yourself with this aspect of the BTR platform.

(Step 3) The MTV Generation

While the term The MTV Generation refers to echo boomers or the Generation X and Y youths of the late 20th Century, it also refers to people heavily influenced by the advent of MTV. In this regard we are all to a certain degree part of the MTV Generation.

Video imagery is a powerful communication force that stimulates the young child watching Saturday morning cartoons to ask Mom and Dad for the latest and greatest toy. It is the gentle yet undeniable part of a one-two punch in which pictures of juicy hamburgers are followed by the hard hitting prompt "aren't you hungry?"

You will have to tune in to my October 15th interview with Dr. Gaby Cora titled "Health in the Boardroom" in which I make reference to the fact that "many of us find ourselves on the unhealthy treadmill of a busy schedule, poor eating habits and an exercise routine that amounts to a power walk to the fridge for a late night snack." These commercials play no small part in stimulating said "power walk."

I could of course go on and on, however I do not think that I have to "paint a picture" in terms of illustrating just how engaging and influential videos are in making a call to action. In the case of a Blog Talk Radio show, the desired action would be to tune in to your broadcast.

This of course goes to the heart of my earlier statement that never before has the capability to produce a high caliber video been so readily available to anyone and everyone through the emergence of social media and in particular on-line tools.

While there are countless video production options available through the Internet, most being free or offered at a nominal monthly cost of a few dollars, the tool or site that I have come to like is One True Video.

As indicated it is a free service, with the option to upgrade to premium features that includes an expanded library of templates costing under $4 per month. Within a matter of minutes I was able to put together a simple video with background music that was fairly impressive.

With increased use I was able to incorporate some pretty amazing special effects that had other BTR hosts commenting and asking where they could go to produce videos for their own shows. Remembering that other hosts are part of your community and not competitors, I was more than happy to provide the link with a few time-saving suggestions based on my experiences with One True Media.

Rather than digress into the finer points of how to create a video, which is better left to on-screen tutorials and familiarity of the service's various bells and whistles through direct use, the point I am making is that a well placed video serves as yet another avenue through which to appeal to your targeted audience. Which tool you ultimately use, and there are many, is up to you. So make certain to check each one out until you find the one you like.

There are a number of tips or guidelines I would follow when producing a video promotion for an upcoming segment including:

- Limit the video's length for promotion for a single segment to between 30 and 60 seconds. Anything longer will likely lose the viewer's interest.

- Single segment promotion should be done for either a special guest or broadcast to which you want to generate increased awareness. When I first started to create videos I enjoyed it so much that I released one for every segment. Besides being time consuming, if you do more than 4 to 6 shows per month the "coolness" factor with the audience will diminish with time to the point where what was once exciting will fall into the same old, same old category. Especially given the fact that after some experimentation you will want to settle on one or two specific formats (including background) music as a means of establishing brand consistency. This of course leads to the next point.

- Instead of creating promotional videos on a per episode basis, try creating one that features highlights from the upcoming month's scheduled shows. For example, I created a video titled "September Sizzles on BTR" in which I provided a cornucopia of information and imagery supported by a catchy, fast-paced tune in the background. Even though the video ran for 1 minute and 46 seconds, which is allowed when you are providing an overview of the month ahead, it helped to stimulate awareness for the PI Window on Business Show in general, showcasing the diversity of topics that we cover and the fact that we are able to draw first rate guests. In the September Sizzles example, I highlighted the fact that we were going to be joined by several bestselling authors – one who was the branding brains behind the Dr. Phil Show (Libby Gill) – a guest panel of industry thought leaders and even a segment on the Buy American policy where I had the opportunity to interview Canada's Trade Minister. Once again, this does not preclude you from using video to promote a single segment, which is something you will want to do for special shows or if you air 4 to 6 shows per month.

- When choosing a video creation tool or platform make certain that it has several features including the ability to quickly and easily upload the finished version to YouTube. YouTube is without a doubt the recognized video resource for the Internet and making your creation available through this venue will lead to an increased number of views. This is especially true if like any other social network, you have built-up the number of contacts in your community through Channel subscriptions.

- One final suggestion is to make certain that you choose the best title for your video that coincides with the interests of the day. For example, I will be doing a special segment on the controversy surrounding the H1N1 virus and the risks associated with using the vaccine. The title for the segment and corresponding video will be "Rolling the Dice with the H1N1 Vaccine." Besides maximizing search engine exposure, the title will by its probing tone likely generate additional traffic as it centers on a topic that is of considerable interest to the population in general.

The key to effectively using video (and audio through tools or services such as Cinch) is to deliver a succinct message within the framework of an entertaining format. Once created, be sure to upload to YouTube, as well as your blog or blogs, and even your main show page on the Blog Talk Radio web site.

You can also share your videos within your various social networking communities through direct post options on YouTube, as well as build up a database of e-mails through which you can forward a video to specific contacts.

(Step 4) On-Demand Player

As I had indicated at the end of the first chapter (page 13), the fact that your BTR show is available on an on-demand basis means that the live broadcast serves as the launching point for the real marketing activity.

When I talk about availability on an on-demand basis, I am of course referring to that fact that all Blog Talk Radio Shows are quite simply recorded and made available shortly after the broadcast ends.

While past shows can be accessed through the Blog Talk Radio web site, BTR also provides you with the embed codes for an attractive on-demand player icon that you can post to your site or share with your guests for posting on their sites. This last point is an important tenet of the perpetual promotion concept as it provides you with the opportunity for establishing an expanded presence in the market as a whole.

The example of the benefits associated with providing and then having your guests post their interview with you on their sites is reflected in my interviews with Libby Gill.

As you will recall, Libby Gill is a bestselling author who also happens to have been the marketing brains behind the Dr. Phil Show. In fact, Dr. Phil has said that "Libby Gill is one of those people who gets it!"

As is often the case with the majority of guests, Libby and I really hit it off resulting in what were highly energetic, informative and entertaining programs. Programs that possess energy and insight are likely the ones that any guest would be more than happy to share within their community of contacts.

In the case of my interviews with Libby, they were posted in the media section of her high traffic web site right next to her other interviews with well-known shows and hosts such as The Big Idea with Donny Deutsch, Oprah & Friends with Jean Chatzky, CNN and The Today Show.

This scenario was replicated with almost every guest including author and Ecademy co-founder Penny Power whose network has grown to a membership of close to half a million people, spanning more than 200 countries. Penny's personal network on Ecademy is close to 25,000 people, so you can imagine how awareness for the show increased through her posting the On-Demand Player on her profile page with the following comment: *"Jon, what an awesome host you were on your Blog Talk Radio show tonight (UK time) - I enjoyed your questions so much, you had that rare skill of digging deep and asking some brilliant questions, showing such depth of insights yourself. Thank you - for anyone who would like to listen, Jon's interview with 3 people- Patrice-Anne Rutledge, and social marketing guru Andrew Ballenthin and myself is here."*

Besides being grateful that PI Window on Business guests such as Libby Gill and Penny Power (both of whom have just recently released their latest books – You Unstuck: Mastering the new rules of risk-taking in work and life by Libby, and Know Me, Like Me, Follow Me by Penny), where gracious in their praise and placement of the show, virtual word-of-mouth sharing such as described above is both invaluable and utterly essential. Especially given the diminishing effectiveness of traditional-type press releases and broadcast advertising practices which actually limits ones ability to get the word out.

Building both a mutually rewarding rapport and relationship with your guests in which you support one another through your respective social networking communities truly reflects David Cushman's assessment of the social media world in which rather than looking toward a "stage" or single point of information dissemination, the emerging world of social media is one where each one of us are looking at one another and determining what we will or will not share in our "communities of purpose."

The ability to share shows through the On-Demand Player is just one of the many vehicles that are available to engage and maintain interconnecting relationships between individual social networking communities.

(Step 5) Syndicated Pings and Other Ways of Reaching Out

There are of course many other tools that are available to both increase your collective reach to the market as a whole, and doing so with greater ease and simplicity.

One such tool through which this can be accomplished is the Ping.fm web site.

Ping.fm is a "simple and free service that makes updating your social networks a snap" by enabling you to write and then simultaneously post to all of your sites with a single click of your mouse.

While some degree of formatting will likely be required, the time it takes to do minor edits is comparatively insignificant when compared with having to do the same post on multiple sites individually.

I personally use Ping.fm to dispatch breaking show news, upcoming events as well as announce polls through what I refer to as the PI Syndicated Ping. Being mindful of formatting as well as the need for the same kind of brevity that is associated with the creation of videos, I try to limit my "Pings" to 140 characters.

Distributed to my social networks such as LinkedIn, Facebook and Twitter, as well as my two blogs on Wordpress, Ping.fm is an incredibly useful tool.

I would remiss if I did not indicate that an increasing number of networks and blogs (including Blog Talk Radio) have some degree of either automatic or manually cross network sharing, or what I often refer to as a cross-pollination capability. While I have certainly used these from time-to-time, Ping.fm seems to have the most extensive list of networking sites which means that it is ideal as a central dispatch service.

Other sites or tools that can help you to extend your reach include StumbleUpon, whose user base of more than 8.5 million people can "discover the best of the web in less time," provides an affordable yet effective means to promote your site by matching your content with the interests of its users.

I recently posted a series of articles on both the Procurement Insights and PI Window on Business Blogs regarding both the shortage and the safety of the H1N1 vaccine. Given the interests of the Procurement Insights blog readership base, I covered the story from the aspects of the challenges associate with production and distribution. With the PI Window on Business blog, I chose to focus my attention on the safety question.

I then entered (re directed) the corresponding links for each article towards the appropriate "unique user interest groups" within StumbleUpon. This meant that the posts would only be read by people who had indicated that these were areas of interest in their StumbleUpon profile.

The value with StumbleUpon besides the spikes in readership is the ability to quickly and easily identify and strategically gain access to unique and specific market interests. After all, why pay a fortune to reach a faceless mass market, when you can zero in on a targeted audience?

There are of course an ever increasing number of other tools that can help you to effectively target and reach out to those in the virtual world whose interests align with the subject matter covered in your Blog Talk Radio show.

Like the aforementioned Twitter, Cinch (which again is the audio Twitter from BTR), and Facebook, each of which have their own amazing tools such as Facebook's ability to create events that can be used to promote an upcoming show by way of direct invitation, there is no shortage of available resources. While I could write a separate book on each one of theses networks and their related functionality in terms of perpetual promotion activities, there are in fact an innumerable number of books that have already been published including author Patrice-Anne Rutledge's "Sams Teach Yourself LinkedIn in 10 minutes." Taking the time to become familiar with these types of resources is an incredibly worthwhile investment.

To end this chapter the way it began, your "perpetual marketing" efforts will "act as an incendiary spark that will ignite a fire within each listener" that will in turn "leverage the viral nature of the social media world to build a sustainable buzz." While only representing a small example of what is available to you through the vast reaches of the Internet, the various tools and web sites referenced above are a cache of invaluable resources that will enable you to put your show and the benefits it provides on the collective radar screens of a significant and interested audience.

At the end of the day, making this connection and sharing with the world around you is ultimately the reason why you decided to host a show in the first place.

# Closing Thoughts

*"You can use your telephone to tape radio shows or perform live, from any place in which there is a good connection, no background noise and where you can talk uninterrupted for the length of the show. Telephone interviews provide inexpensive exposure because the producer will call you, typically."*

*From the 2003 Writing-World.com article "Promoting Your Book Through Telephone Interviews" by Brian Jud*

Even though author, speaker and book marketing consultant Brian Jud was talking about traditional or conventional radio in making the above statement, he obviously recognized the potential of what would become Blog Talk Radio.

Beyond the advent of exciting new innovations including the utilization of Skype or a similar-type program to connect with anyone from around the world without incurring the long distance fees associated with using the telephone, the ability to extend marketing activities beyond the live broadcast for a particular show would be of interest to Jud.

After all Jud, who ironically wrote a book titled "Perpetual Promotion (How to Contact Producers and Create Media Appearances)," would undoubtedly recognize the seemingly limitless opportunities with Internet radio.

In the forward for Your Show Will Go Live in 5 Seconds I indicated that the purpose of this book was to "share with you my experiences and insights in creating and hosting a show that informs, empowers and enriches your audience, your guests and yes, even yourself."

In the process it was and is my sincerest hope that your investment in these 10 Chapters would "in some small way help you to walk through your door of what will ultimately become your greatest adventure." In essence help you to both realize and seize the opportunity to be heard in an increasingly small and crowded world of diverse interests and competing voices.

If I have been able to help you to do this, even with just a single idea that you would not have otherwise considered then my time and effort in writing Your Show Will Go Live in 5 Seconds will have been worth it.

That said I will close this book with the same words that I use to close each and every PI Window on Business Show . . . "Thank you for investing what is the most important asset that you have, which is your time."

# Appendix A – PI Social Media References & Resources

The PI Window on Business Show:

Reaching an estimated 1 million syndicated subscribers worldwide every month, The PI Social Media Network is internationally recognized for its ability to identify, structure and disseminate the ideas and visions that are reshaping the emerging global enterprise – (http://www.blogtalkradio.com/Jon-Hansen)

The PI Window on Business Blog:

What is bound to become the definitive on-air show for the business professional, PI Window on Business will discuss provocative subjects from the world of business including the global supply chain community.

The regularly scheduled 60 minute segments as well as our 90-minute specials will feature thought provoking and entertaining guests from the world of business and politics, bestselling authors as well as industry thought leaders.

We look forward to you joining us on-air and live on the PI Window on Business Blog Talk Radio throughout the week between 12:30 and 1:30 PM EDT – http://piwindowonbusiness.wordpress.com/)

Procurement Insights Blog:

We live in a Knowledge-based World!

Without a doubt we have greater access to more information than at any other point in history. The challenges we face however are not linked to the volume of information, nor are they tied to the vehicles we use to corral the diverse streams of dynamic data. Our biggest challenge is effectively sifting through the chaos of misinformation and self-serving pontification to uncover the true jewels of insight that can positively influence our world and transform our lives and businesses.

This is the cornerstone of Procurement Insights' "mission," which is to engage, inform and empower our growing readership base through thought provoking articles and a growing library of industry specific white papers.

In association with The PI Social Media Network's Blog Talk Radio program PI Window on Business and the newly launched PI Window on Business Blog, Procurement Insights is committed to being a premier supply chain information source in the market – (http://procureinsights.wordpress.com/)

Light of Love Blog:

From a personal perspective, I had cause to recently consider my own journey to the cross, and the Christian life I have come to enthusiastically embrace.

For many of us, the transformation of our hearts and lives is associated with a gradual series of events that evolve over a lifetime of experiences –

(http://savannahmaria.wordpress.com/)

# Appendix B – Blog Talk Radio Resources

What is Blog Talk Radio?

Blog Talk Radio allows anyone, anywhere the ability to host a live, Internet Talk Radio show, simply by using a telephone and a computer.

Blog Talk Radio's unique technology and seamless integration with leading social networks such as Facebook, Twitter, and Ning, empowers citizen broadcasters to create and share their original content, their voices and their opinions in a public worldwide forum.

Today, Blog Talk Radio is the largest and fastest-growing social radio network on the Internet. A truly democratized medium, Blog Talk Radio has tens of thousands of hosts and millions of listeners tuning in and joining the conversation each month. Many businesses also utilize the platform as a tool to extend their brands and join the conversation on the social web.

Join the Conversation:
http://www.blogtalkradio.com/register.aspx?type=listener

Start a Conversation:
http://www.blogtalkradio.com/register.aspx?type=Host

Learn about Blog Talk Radio's
http://www.blogtalkradio.com/advertising.aspx

Blog Talk Radio Learning Center:

Tutorials, tips, and techniques to expand your Internet Radio Voice - (http://www.blogtalkradio.com/faq.aspx)

Blog Talk Radio 101:

Welcome to Blog Talk Radio 101! Here you'll find screencast tutorials to help get started listening, hosting, and networking. To watch our screencast tutorials, click on the tutorial name below – (http://www.blogtalkradio.com/BTR101.aspx)

Contact Blog Talk Radio:

(http://www.blogtalkradio.com/ContactUs.aspx)

# Appendix C – Internet References & Resources

Social Networks:

Ecademy – (http://www.ecademy.com/)

Twitter – (http://twitter.com/)

LinkedIn – (http://www.linkedin.com/)

Facebook – (http://www.facebook.com/)

Cinch – (http://www.cinchcast.com/about.aspx)

The Perfect Networker – (http://www.perfectnetworker.com/)

Inquisix Reputation Network – (http://inquisix.com/)

Media Resources:

The Future Buzz – (http://thefuturebuzz.com/)

StumbleUpon – (http://www.stumbleupon.com/)

Ping.fm – (http://www.ping.fm/)

Internet Television/Video:

USTREAM – (http://www.ustream.tv/)

Blog TV – (http://www.blogtv.com/)

ooVoo – (http://www.oovoo.com/)

Video Resources:

One True Media – (http://www.onetruemedia.com/otm_site/home)

YouTube – (http://www.youtube.com/)

# Acknowledgements

As I had stated in this book's forward, even though the profession of one's faith is sometimes frowned upon in the realms of the business world, my faith (or to be more accurate God's love and guidance) is the reason I am where I am today.

Falling from what some would consider to be the heights of privilege in which I was for all intents and purposes detached somewhat from the real world, to one in which I have discovered my true calling which is writing and yes, even hosting a radio show, I cannot think of any better scenario for moving into the latter half of my life.

Without God's loving "motivation" through difficult circumstances I would never have picked-up a pen (or typed a keyboard) to write, let alone host a show on Blog Talk Radio. For this I am eternally grateful and look forward to serving God in whatever capacity He deems appropriate.

Then of course there is my family.

Anyone who has ever written a single word knows that one's family is the enduring support system that enables one of its members to pursue their best regardless of the task being undertaken.

Writing a book is not easy work to be certain. Maintaining a loving and supportive home which adapts to the unusual schedule of a writer's literary spark is in many ways more challenging.

For this reason I would like to thank Jennifer who over the years has become my greatest passion next to serving God. She is the one who with enduring perseverance has always made the suggestion that I write a book. When circumstances made this endeavor possible and even necessary, she was there to answer the call thus putting action to her words. I will love you always for this, and for who you are.

I would be remiss if I did not also acknowledge my two children Savannah Maria, who is almost 5 and Pierce Christian who on the date this book will be officially released – November 2nd – will turn 2.

Being a close family, the greatest sacrifice a child can make is willingly surrendering time with a parent. While I did all that I could to maintain a regular presence, I know that you wanted so much more but were willing to wait until Daddy finished his book. The exclamation point to our children's understanding came the day I announced that the book was done. Savannah came to me and said Daddy I am so proud of you! Those words are a treasure of love that will remain with me always, as will the experience of writing this, my first book.

# About the Author

Jon William Hansen was born in Winnipeg, Manitoba on July 21, 1959.

Now living in Buckingham, Quebec which is a small town of approximately 12,000 people that is 20 minutes outside of Canada's Capital, Ottawa, Jon and his family Jennifer, Savannah Maria, Pierce Christian and their two dogs Capone and Psang, Psang live a peaceful and satisfying life. Beyond the obvious passion for social media, family activites center on volunteering at the local Legion where Jennifer is 2$^{nd}$ Vice president, and pursuing both family and individual interests which includes art and dance.

In May 2001 Jon sold his company for $12 million dollars – mostly shares and debentures, only to see the dot com bust erode away his personal wealth to practically nothing by 2007. This as it turns out was the catalyst that caused him to pursue his present endeavor in the world of social media.

Today, the PI Social Media Network is viewed as being one of the top networks in the industry in terms of innovation and quality of content. The flagship Procurement Insights is actually the number one sponsored blog in its industry sector in total number of sponsors, and industry pundits rate the PI Window on Business Show as one of the most popular in North America.

Besides writing more than 350 articles and white papers, Jon is also a highly regarded speaker addressing audiences of all sizes ranging from 10 to 20 people in a seminar to giving keynote addresses to 400 attendees at major conferences.

Prior to completing this book, Jon had finalized the agreement to write a second book on the emergence of the So Act social network. This second book is scheduled for release in February 2010.

Made in the USA
Lexington, KY
22 June 2010